Music for Analysis

*Examples from the Common Practice Period
and the Twentieth Century*

SIXTH EDITION

Thomas Benjamin
Peabody Conservatory of the Johns Hopkins University

Michael Horvit   Robert Nelson
Moores School of Music, University of Houston

Exv. of sequence
piece no.
107
160
93
373
372

New York   Oxford
OXFORD UNIVERSITY PRESS
2007

Oxford University Press, Inc., publishes works that further Oxford University's
objective of excellence in research, scholarship, and education.

Oxford   New York
Auckland   Cape Town   Dar es Salaam   Hong Kong   Karachi
Kuala Lampur   Madrid   Melbourne   Mexico City   Nairobi
New Delhi   Shanghai   Taipei   Toronto

With offices in
Argentina   Austria   Brazil   Chile   Czech Republic   France   Greece
Guatemala   Hungary   Italy   Japan   Poland   Portugal   Singapore
South Korea   Switzerland   Thailand   Turkey   Ukraine   Vietnam

Copyright © 2007 by Oxford University Press, Inc.

Published by Oxford University Press, Inc.
198 Madison Avenue, New York, New York 10016
http://www.oup.com

ISBN–13: 978-0-19-518815-8

ISBN: 0-19-518815-2

Printing number: 9 8 7 6 5 4 3 2 1

Printed in the United States of America
on acid-free paper

Contents

Part I   Diatonic Materials

SUGGESTIONS FOR DISCUSSION

1. Tonic Triad

Questions for Analysis

2. Dominant Triad in Root Position

Questions for Analysis

3. Dominant Seventh and Ninth in Root Position

Questions for Analysis

Model Analysis

4. Subdominant Triad in Root Position

Questions for Analysis

5. Cadential Tonic Six-Four Chord
Questions for Analysis

6. Tonic, Subdominant, and Dominant Triads in First Inversion
Questions for Analysis

7. Supertonic Triad
Questions for Analysis

8. Inversions of the Dominant Seventh Chord
Questions for Analysis

9. Linear (Embellishing) Six-Four Chords
Questions for Analysis

10. Submediant and Mediant Triads
Questions for Analysis

11. Leading Tone Triad
Questions for Analysis

15. Other Diatonic Seventh Chords
Questions for Analysis

16. Complete Pieces for Analysis I
Checklist for Analysis

Part II   Chromatic Materials
SUGGESTIONS FOR DISCUSSION

17. Secondary (Applied, Borrowed) Dominants
Questions for Analysis
Model Analysis

18. Modulation to Closely Related Keys

Questions for Analysis

MODULATION TO DOMINANT

MODULATION TO RELATIVE MAJOR

MODULATION TO OTHER CLOSELY RELATED KEYS

19. Complete Pieces for Analysis II

Checklist for Analysis

20. Linear (Embellishing) Diminished Seventh Chords

Questions for Analysis

21. Neapolitan Triad

Questions for Analysis

22. Augmented Sixth Chords, Submediant Degree as Lowest Note

Questions for Analysis

ITALIAN

23. Augumented Sixth Chords, Other Scale Degrees as Lowest Note

Questions for Analysis

24. Augumented Sixth Chords, Other Uses

Question for Analysis

25. Other Means of Modulation

Question for Analysis

26. Ninth Chords

Questions for Analysis

DOMINANT NINTHS

SECONDARY DOMINANT NINTHS

NONDOMINANT NINTHS

27. Extended Linear Usages

Questions for Analysis

28. Complete Pieces for Analysis III
Checklist for Analysis

29. Examples of Counterpoint
Questions for Analysis

*Additional Examples for the Study
of Contrapuntual Techniques*

Part III   Contemporary Materials
SUGGESTIONS FOR DISCUSSION

30. Extended and Altered Tertian Harmony
Questions for Analysis

35. Polyharmony and Polytonality

Questions for Analysis

36. Free Atonality

Questions for Analysis

37. Twelve-Tone Serialism

Questions for Analysis

38. Music Since 1945

Questions for Analysis

39. Complete Pieces for Analysis IV

Suggestion for Analysis

CD Track List

Track 1.
  2. CZERNY, *Sonatina, op. 792, no. 8*
  7. CHOPIN, *Valse (Posthumous)* (:06)

Track 2.
  10. MOZART, *Rondo*
  11. KUHNAU, *Biblical Sonata No. 1: Victory Dance and Festival* (:10)
  12. BEETHOVEN, *Für Elise* (:23)

Track 3.
  16. WEBER, *German Dance*
  17. MOZART, *Sonata, K. 332* (:09)
  20. HAYDN, *Sonata in E major, Hob. XVI: 13* (:22)
  23. SCHUBERT, *Ländler* (:30)
  24. SCHUBERT, *Valses Nobles, op. 77* (:43)

Track 4.
  26. SCHEIDT, *Bergamasca*
  27. SCHUMANN, *Faschingsschwank aus Wien, op. 26, no. 3: Scherzino* (:18)
  28. CHOPIN, *Mazurka, op. 17, no. 1* (:31)
  31. SCHUBERT, *Impromptu, op. 90, no. 4, D. 899* (:47)
  33. BEETHOVEN, *Seven Country Dances, no. 7* (1:10)
  34. SCHUBERT, *Ländler* (1:31)

Track 5.
  35. SCHUBERT, *Valses Sentimentales, op. 50, no. 18*

Track 6.
  39. BACH, *Lobt Gott, ihr Christen, allzugleich*
  41. MOZART, *Sonata, K. 332* (:13)
  42. HAYDN, *Sonata in D major, Hob. XVI:37* (:24)
  46. MOZART, *Sonata, K. 570* (:36)
  48. COUPERIN, *Le Petit Rien* (1:03)

Track 7.
  50. ANONYMOUS, *Dir, dir, Jehovah, will ich singen*
  51. SCHUBERT, *Waltz, op. 9, no. 3, D. 365* (:15)
  52. BEETHOVEN, *Six Variations on "Nel cor più non mi sento"* (:26)
  57. CHOPIN, *Mazurka, op. 33, no. 2* (:39)

Track 8.
  59. J. C. F. BACH, *Nun danket alle Gott*
  60. HAYDN, *Sonata in C major, Hob. XVI: 35* (:25)
  63. BEETHOVEN, *Sonata, op. 31, no. 3* (:35)
  66. KUHLAU, *Sonatina, op. 20, no. 1* (:50)
  68. BEETHOVEN, *Minuet in C* (1:01)

Track 9.
  70. SCHUBERT, *Valses Sentimentales, op. 50, no. 1, D. 779*
  71. MOZART, *Rondo, K. 485* (:12)
  73. SCHUBERT, *Waltz, op. 9, no. 1, D. 365* (:39)
  74. KUHLAU, *Sonatina, op. 88, no. 3* (:48)
  76. BEETHOVEN, *Sonatina in G major* (1:00)
  79. HAYDN, *Sonata in D major, Hob. XVI: 37* (1:18)
  80. BEETHOVEN, *Contradanse* (1:35)

Track 10.
  85. CRÜGER, *Herzliebster Jesu, was hast du verbrochen*
  86. ANONYMOUS, *Dir, dir, Jehovah, will ich singen* (:22)
  87. BACH, *Schmücke dich, o liebe Seele* (:44)
  89. MOZART, *Sonata, K. 545* (1:14)
  96. MOZART, *Sonata, K. 283* (1:24)
  97. J. C. F. BACH, *Menuet* (1:42)
  100. BRAHMS, *Romance, op. 118, no. 5* (2:03)
  101. SCHUMANN, *Phantasiestücke, op. 12, no. 4, Grillen* (2:24)

Track 11.
  105. BACH, *Aus meines Herzens Grunde*
  106. SCHUMANN, *Album for the Young, op. 68: Soldatenmarsch* (:25)
  108. HAYDN, *Sonata in E♭ major, Hob. XVI: 49* (:33)
  109. HAYDN, *Sonatina in D major, Hob. XVI: 4* (:45)
  110. MOZART, *Sonata, K. 280* (:58)

Track 12.
  116. A. SCARLATTI, *Folia*
  117. MATTHESON, *Minuet* (:18)
  118. MOZART, *Sonata, K. 310* (:28)
  122. HAYDN, *Sonatina in C major, Hob. XVI: 7* (:34)

Track 13.
  129. ANONYMOUS, *Herr, wie du willst, so schick's mit mir*
  132. GRIEG, *Voegtersang* (:29)
  135. MOZART, *Sonata, K. 310* (:51)
  138. BEETHOVEN, *Sonata, op. 14, no. 2* (1:03)

Track 14.
  143. MOZART, *Sonata, K. 457*

Track 15.
  144. SCHUMANN, *Carnaval, op. 9: Chiarina*

Track 16.
  145. BRAHMS, *Ballade, op. 10, no. 4*

Preface to the Sixth Edition

In the belief that musical study should focus on the music itself, we have assembled the sixth edition of *Music for Analysis* to provide students with ready access to a far-ranging variety of music. The stylistic and historical breadth, as well as the systematic format, run parallel to our *Techniques and Materials of Music* (Thomson/Schirmer, Sixth Edition, 2003), but also allow you to use this anthology with many other theory textbooks. With the addition of a significant number of complete pieces, including an entire Mozart Sonata, this anthology now also can be used in traditional form and analysis courses. To assist those instructors teaching a form course, an Index of Complete Pieces has been added. This index contains 105 selections, from small forms to large-scale works. A Textbook Correlation Chart for standard theory books currently in print appears in Appendix C; books dealing with form can be found in the bibliography in Appendix B.

Music for Analysis moves progressively from the techniques and materials of the common practice period through the twentieth century. In this sixth edition:

- Harmonic content forms the organizing principle and builds cumulatively and systematically.
- Musical selections:
  - focus clearly on one chord or technique and use music within the range of competent pianists.
  - illustrate the standard usage and idiomatic procedures of historical periods from the seventeenth through twenty-first centuries.
  - cover a wide variety of textures and styles.
  - draw from chamber music, vocal music, keyboard music, and orchestral music—in piano reduction, short score, or full score.
  - draw from American popular music and jazz throughout the book.
  - include excerpts of at least period length as well as many complete works.
- The many excerpts organized by harmonic content make *Music for Analysis* the ideal anthology for traditional harmony courses, but *Music for Analysis* is now an ideal resource for traditional form courses. The many longer excerpts illustrate small forms such as simple binary, and the numerous complete pieces illustrate all the common large forms. This edition adds clear examples of simple ternary form, new examples illustrating the various variation forms, and a complete Mozart Sonata for study of sonata-allegro and rondo form. An index of all the complete pieces has been added for easy reference.
- Unit 29 has been expanded with additional complete pieces and now includes contrapuntal examples from composers other than Bach. At the end of the unit is a list of a considerable number of contrapuntal examples found throughout the book.
- Part III presents a clear and systematic illustration of specific techniques and styles found in contemporary music. The sixth edition adds additional complete pieces, including a movement of a Hindemith piano sonata and the Theme and Variations from Stravinsky's *Sonata for Two Pianos.*

- The "Questions for Analysis" found in each unit guide study and discussion and remind the student of the comprehensive nature of analysis. The detailed checklist and model analysis in Appendix A provide a useful summary for the student learning to analyze music. There are now additional model analyses appearing in Units 3 and 17. These model analyses show the detail expected at each level of study and reinforce the desired goal of a comprehensive analysis of the music as opposed to a simple harmonic analysis and the mere parsing of the phrases.
- A detailed Index of Composers facilitates the study of a particular composer or style and makes a given selection easy to find.

Movement and measure numbers are provided for excerpts that do not begin a work; longer excerpts and complete pieces now have measure numbers provided for ease of reference when discussing the music. Unless otherwise indicated, the excerpt begins on measure 1. In certain cases, a musical selection may contain chords that anticipate later units. In these cases, because we believe that the significance of the selection justifies its inclusion, we provide an analysis of the particular chords. Inevitably, certain selections will suggest alternative analyses; we consider it best to allow the instructor to determine the preferred analysis.

We wish again to thank Edward Haymes for his help with the translations. For their very helpful advice toward the sixth edition of *Music for Analysis* we would like to thank Ellon Carpenter, Arizona State University; James Dapogny, University of Michigan; Jolene Davis, University of Georgia; Stephanie Dickinson, University of Central Arkansas; John Drumheller, University of Colorado; Cynthia Folio, Temple University; David Goodman, Santa Monica College; Thom Hasenpflug, Idaho State University; Charles Leinberger, UTEP Department of Music; W. Thomas McKenney, University of Missouri-Columbia; Cindy Moyer, Humboldt State University; Raymond G. Riley, Alma College; C. Scott Smith, Ohio University; and Scott Charles Spiegelberg, Indiana University.

This edition of the anthology includes a new audio CD of more than 140 examples from the text played on the piano, harpsichord, or organ by Dr. Rosilee Walker Russell, Artist-in-Residence at the University of Arkansas - Fort Smith. We hope this listening tool makes the musical examples easier for students to access.

We also wish to thank Shanta Sivasingham and Andrew Davis for their help in revising the Textbook Correlation Chart, Adele Lynch for checking movement and measure numbers, and Nedra Booker for helping with permissions.

T.B.   M.H.   R.N.

Suggestions for Using This Book

1. We urge the class to discuss all aspects of the music being analyzed–not to focus solely, for example, on harmonic content. Constant reference should be made in class discussion to such matters as motivic unity and derivation, melodic construction, counterpoint, cadence and phrase structure, texture, idiom, rhythm, and the like. Suggestions for Discussion precede each large section of the book, and each unit has Questions for Analysis. Model analyses appear at the beginning of Units 3 and 17, and a comprehensive Checklist for Analysis and model analysis is provided in Appendix A. These serve as a guide to the teacher and models for the student. Instructors are, of course, free to choose their own analytic approaches and terminologies.

2. It is important to emphasize the organic nature of music so as to avoid limiting class discussion to mere surface description. The interactions of line, rhythm, phrase, and harmony should be investigated. Many complete pieces are provided throughout to allow the students some experience with formal analysis.

3. The instructor should insist that students listen to the assigned music before doing an analysis and should always play the music in class both before and after discussion. We recommend the use of student performers whenever possible. Further, all of the examples in the anthology are drawn from standard literature. Most keyboard examples, including those for piano, harpsichord, and organ, are included on the accompanying CD. All other examples should be readily available on record or CD in university and college listening laboratories.

4. Examples of contrapuntal textures are found throughout the anthology. Complete pieces using contrapuntal techniques are designated with an asterisk in the Index of Complete Pieces.

5. Such important matters as performance practice, style, and historical context should be discussed in class. Clarification of problems of performance through analysis is often of interest to the student and should be undertaken.

6. The music in this anthology can be used not only for analysis but also for ear-training, sight-reading, score-reading, and transposition practice.

7. Users of our *Techniques and Materials of Music* (Thomson/Schirmer, Sixth Edition, 2003) will note that the organization of this anthology closely parallels that of our textbook. The materials provided in Part V of *Techniques and Materials* will be particularly helpful to these instructors; pertinent units in the book include those on cadence and phrase structure, motive, sequence, melody, and small forms.

I. Diatonic Materials

Suggestions for Discussion

Though the music in this section is organized by harmonic vocabulary, it is not enough to simply label the chords with roman numerals and move on. In fact, in those excerpts where the harmonic content is simpler, analysis should focus on all the other aspects of the music, including such basic concepts as harmonic rhythm and the way the voicing and voice-leading is affected by the texture of the music. Harmonic analysis is only the first basic step to understanding and analyzing the structure of a piece of music.

Aspects to Consider

From the very beginning, analysis should include considerations of phrase, period, and cadence; motivic structure; melodic shape; and how all work together to create the musical form. To aid in the analytic process, units are prefaced with questions meant to guide your consideration and analysis of the music. These questions are cumulative and should be considered in all subsequent units.

- Always play the music first, and again after analysis; the *sound* is what matters, and sometimes the eye can be misled. We stress the importance of *hearing* each example in class.
- Always work from large to small. The largest formal units (overall form, structural pitches, cadence, phrase, and periodic structure) should be understood before tackling the details (motives, rhythmic detail, harmony, nonharmonic tones, and so on).
- Always put the music in a context: Who wrote it, when, and what's the nature of the style? What clues about the style does the music give us?
- How does what we have discovered about any particular excerpt or piece help us perform that piece more musically and intelligently?

1. Tonic Triad

Questions for Analysis

1. How is the triad expressed, both melodically and harmonically?
2. How does the texture affect the voicing?
3. Given the lack of a harmonic progression, how are phraselike structures established and articulated?
4. Are successive motives or "phrases" related by sequence, repetition, or other means?

1. Sonatina in G major, Hob. XVI: 8
I

2. Sonatina, op. 792, no. 8
I

3. Le Coq d'Or: Hymn to the Sun
m. 3

Note: Movement and measure numbers are given throughout. Where no measure number is given, the excerpt begins on measure 1.

4. Leonora Overture No. 2, op. 72
m. 37

Beethoven

5. Trio, op. 70, no. 2
I

Beethoven

Violin

Cello

Piano

6. Polens Grabgesang, op. 74

Chopin

Von dem Baum im Wet - ter san - ken al - le Blät - ter!

In the storm, all the leaves fell from the tree.

7. Valse (Posthumous)

Chopin

8. Symphony No. 5, op. 67
II, m. 230

Beethoven

9. Carnival

Allegro

Couperin

2. Dominant Triad in Root Position

Questions for Analysis
1. Which dominant chords are clearly cadential? What other devices (melodic, rhythmic) help to establish cadence points?
2. Consider the harmonic voice-leading. How does texture affect the details of the chord connections? Consider particularly the Alberti bass in Example 10 and the arpeggiations in Example 12.

---

10. Rondo

Mozart

---

11. Biblical Sonata No. 1: Victory Dance and Festival

Kuhnau

12. Für Elise

Poco moto

Beethoven

13. Album for the Young, op. 68: Reiterstück

Kurz und bestimmt

Schumann

14. Euryanthe, op. 81: Overture

Allegro marcato, con molto fuoco

Weber

15. Symphony No. 5, op. 67
I, m. 484

Allegro con brio

Beethoven

3. Dominant Seventh and Ninth* in Root Position

Questions for Analysis

1. Where do tendency tones occur? How are they resolved?
2. How does texture affect the voicing and connection of the chords?
3. Where do cadences occur? How are they established?
4. Does the harmonic rhythm change at cadential points?
5. Do phrases form periods? If so, which type?
6. Are the phrases within each period equal in length?

Model Analysis

Beethoven, *Piano Sonata, op. 31, no.2*

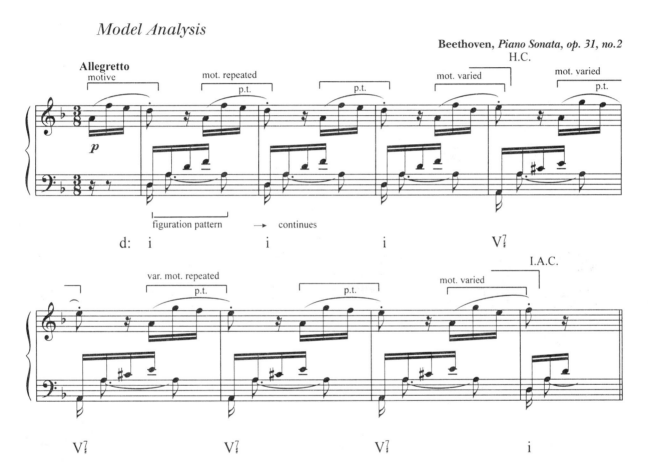

Observations:

A. Form: two four-measure phrases, a|a' forming a period in which the same motive appears in both phrases but is altered in the second phrase to fit the underlying harmony. The structural harmony supports the two-part structure: i →V answered and balanced by V→i.

B. The excerpt is highly continuous in its rhythmic flow and highly unified in its motivic material (one motivic idea and one figuration pattern).

*For additional examples of the dominant ninth, see Part II, Unit 26.

C. Harmonic rhythm is slow and regular:

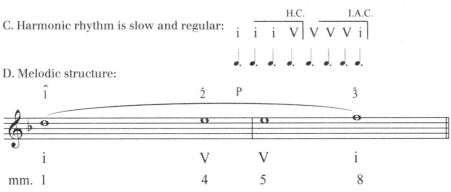

D. Melodic structure:

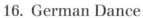

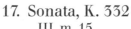

P = passing motion. Carets over numbers refer to scale degrees.

E. See also Appendix A, p. 503.

16. German Dance

Weber

17. Sonata, K. 332
III, m. 15

Allegro

Mozart

18. Wiegenlied, op. 98, no. 2

Schubert

Schla - fe, schla - fe, hol - der, sü - ßer Kna - be,

lei - se wiegt dich dei - ner Mut - ter Hand;

Sleep, sleep, dear sweet child; thy Mother's hand gently rocks thee.

19. Rigoletto, Act I, no. 2

Verdi

Que-sta o quel - la per me pa - ri so - no a quan-

t'al - tre d'in - tor - no, _____ d'in - tor - no mi ve - do,

del mio co - re _____ l'im - pe - ro non ce - do _____

me - glio ad u - na, _____ che ad al - tra bel - tà.

This one or that one, it's all the same to me. As to the others I see around me,
I don't yield my heart more to one beauty than to another.

———————

20. Sonata in E major, Hob. XVI: 13
III, m. 15

Presto

Haydn

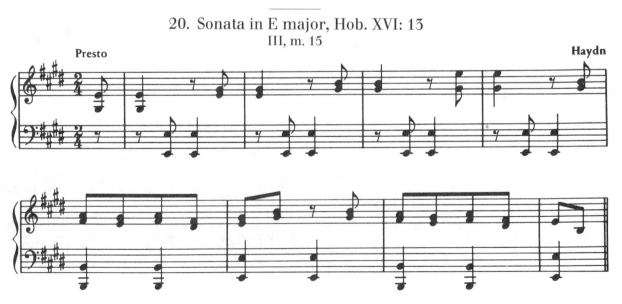

21. Symphony No. 4, op. 60
I, m. 177

Allegro vivace

Beethoven

sempre *f*

22. Oberon: Overture
m. 22

Allegro con fuoco

Weber

23. Ländler

Schubert

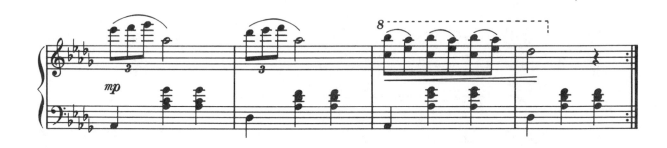

24. Valses Nobles, op. 77

Schubert

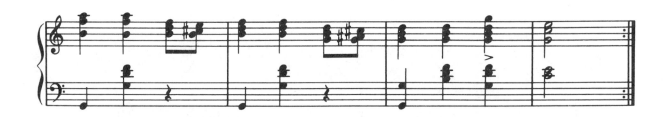

25. Valse

Mozart

$\left[I\,{}^{6}_{4} \right]$

3. DOMINANT SEVENTH AND NINTH IN ROOT POSITION   17

4. Subdominant Triad in Root Position

Questions for Analysis

1. What is the explanation for all the accidentals in Example 30?
2. What is the formal design of the complete pieces (Examples 33 and 34)?
3. How does motive contribute to the form of these pieces?

---

26. Bergamasca

---

27. Faschingsschwank aus Wien, op. 26, no. 3: Scherzino
m. 86

28. Mazurka, op. 17, no. 1

29. Egmont Overture, op. 84
m. 82

30. Rigoletto, Act I, no. 7

Verdi

Gilda: What sadness! what sadness! have rung such bitter tears.
Rigoletto: You alone remain in misery...

31. Impromptu, op. 90, no. 4, D. 899
m. 88

Allegretto

Schubert

32. Look for the Silver Lining

Burthen (*slowly*)

Kern

Look for_____ the sil - ver lin - ing_____

When - e'er a cloud ap - pears in the

blue._____

33. Seven Country Dances, no. 7

Allegro

Beethoven

34. Ländler

Schubert

5. Cadential Tonic Six-Four Chord

Questions for Analysis

1. Do any of the examples in this unit contain phrase groups or double periods?
2. How is the cadential tonic six-four chord introduced and resolved? Consider aspects of doubling and voice-leading as well as those of rhythm and meter.

35

35. Valses Sentimentales, op. 50, no. 18
m. 10

Schubert

36

36. Mazurka, op. 24, no. 3

Moderato, con anima

Chopin

37. Lucia di Lammermoor, Act II, no. 6
m. 344

Donizetti

(Lucy)
Io son tan - to sven - tu - ra - ta,

(Henry)
Quel - la scu - re san - gui - no - sa

che la mor - te è un ben per me, sì,___ la

sta - rà sem - pre in - nan - zi a te, sem - pre,

mor - te, sì,___ la mor - te è un ben per___ me, sì,___ la

sem - pre, sem - pre, sem - pre in - nan - zi a te, sem - pre,

5. CADENTIAL TONIC SIX-FOUR CHORD   25

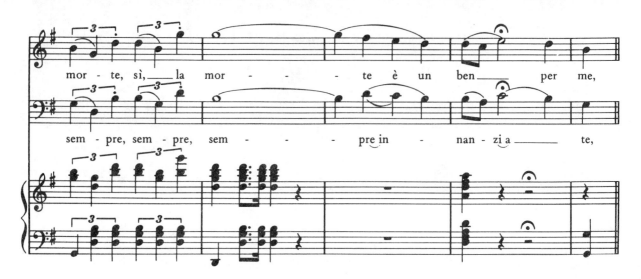

Lucy: I am so wretched that death is a blessing for me, yes, death is a blessing for me.

Henry: That bloody axe will always be before you.

38. Trio, op. 97

6. Tonic, Subdominant, and Dominant Triads in First Inversion

Questions for Analysis
1. Where do chords in inversion occur?
2. How does the inversion of these chords affect the bass line?

39. Lobt Gott, ihr Christen, allzugleich

40. Bastien und Bastienne, K. 46B, no. 9

Go on! You're telling me a fib. Bastienne, don't deceive me.

---

41. Sonata, K. 332
I, m. 145

Allegro

Mozart

---

42. Sonata in D major, Hob. XVI: 37
III, m. 114

Presto ma non troppo

Haydn

*See Chapter 9.

43. Abendempfindung, K. 523

Mozart

It's evening. The sun has faded.

44. Symphony No. 5, op. 67

IV

Beethoven

45. Fidelio, Act I, no. 9
m. 34

Beethoven

46. Sonata, K. 570

Mozart

Which notes in the bass line of the example below are clearly roots or thirds and which are merely passing tones?

47. Elijah, op. 70, no. 29
m. 70

Mendelssohn

He, watch - ing Is - - - - ra - el,

He, watch - ing Is - ra - el,

He, watch- - - ing

He, watch - - ing Is - - ra -

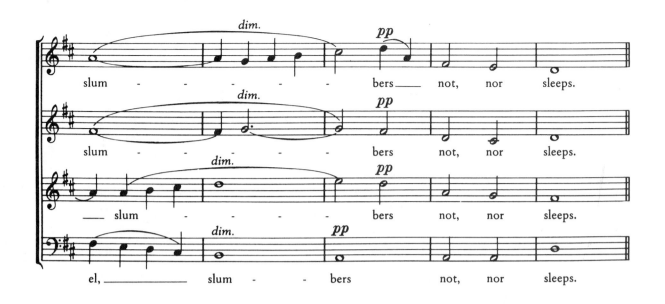

slum - - - - - bers___ not, nor sleeps.

slum - - - - bers not, nor sleeps.

___ slum - - - bers not, nor sleeps.

el, _____ slum - - bers not, nor sleeps.

48. Le Petit Rien
m. 67

Allegro   Couperin

ii

49. Les Fifres

Vif   Dandrieu

7. Supertonic Triad

Questions for Analysis

1. How is the supertonic triad introduced and resolved? Which note is doubled in the ii6?
2. Where do cadences occur? How are they established? Do phrases form periods?

---

50. Dir, dir, Jehovah, will ich singen

Anon.

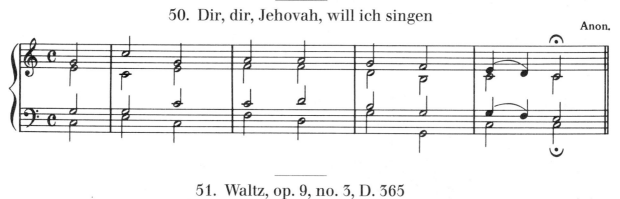

---

51. Waltz, op. 9, no. 3, D. 365

Schubert

---

52. Six Variations on "Nel cor più non mi sento"

Beethoven

53. Die Zauberflöte, K. 620, Act II, no. 21

m. 584

Mozart

Ring, little bells, ring. Bring my maiden here.

54. Zwei Leichen

Chopin

muss - ten sich mei - den und von ein - an - der ge - hen.

$$V7/iv \qquad ii^{ø6}_5$$

Two lovers were kept from each other and had to part.

55. Trio, op. 121A

Allegretto

Beethoven

Violin

Cello

Piano

Allegretto

56. Rigoletto, Act II, no. 14

Verdi

Yes, revenge, terrible revenge, is this soul's only desire.

57. Mazurka, op. 33, no. 2

Vivace   Chopin

58. Sonata in E minor, Hob. XVI: 34

II

Adagio   Haydn

8. Inversions of the Dominant Seventh Chord

Questions for Analysis
1. Where do tendency tones occur? How are they resolved?
2. Do inversons of dominant sevenths occur at cadence points? If so, how does this affect the relative strength of the cadence?

59. Nun danket alle Gott

J. C. F. Bach

60. Sonata in C major, Hob. XVI: 35
I

Haydn

61. Le donne sur balcone

Paisiello

Le don-ne sul bal - co — ne   so be - ne in-do-vi -

nar.   I gio - va - ni al can - to - ne   so me-glio stuz-zi - car.

The ladies on the balcony I know well how to evaluate,
The young men on the corner I know better how to tease.

---

62. Quartet, K. 464

Allegro   Mozart

---

63. Sonata, op. 31, no. 3
II

Allegretto vivace   Beethoven

64. Sarabande I, vol. I

Rameau

ii°7

65. Trio in C major, Hob. XV: 3

Haydn*

Violin

Cello

Piano

*Possibly by Pleyel.

66. Sonatina, op. 20, no. 1

Allegro

Kuhlau

67. Symphony No. 2, op. 36

Allegro molto

Beethoven

68. Minuet in C

Moderato

Beethoven

*See Part I, Unit 9.

9. Linear (Embellishing) Six-Four Chords

Questions for Analysis

1. Which chords are clearly functional? Which are linear?
2. What combinations of nonharmonic tones create the linear chords?

69. Concerto No. 1 for Piano, op. 15

Beethoven

70. Valses Sentimentales, op. 50, no. 1, D. 779

Schubert

71. Rondo, K. 485

Mozart

72. Quartet, op. 3, no. 5

Haydn

73. Waltz, op. 9, no. 1, D. 365

Schubert

74. Sonatina, op. 88, no. 3
III

Kuhlau

75. Symphony No. 35, K. 385

Mozart

76. Sonatina in G major
I, m. 25

Moderato

Beethoven

77. Symphony No. 7, op. 92
I, m. 63

Vivace

Beethoven

78. Symphony No. 41, K. 551
I

Allegro vivace   Mozart

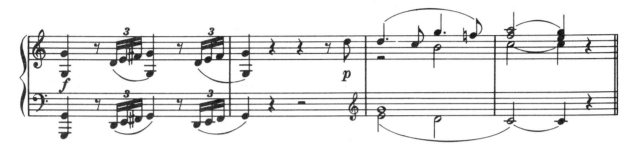

79. Sonata in D major, Hob. XVI: 37
I

Allegro con brio   Haydn

80. Contradanse

Allegro

Beethoven

81. Passacaglia

Buxtehude

6

82. Symphony No. 3, op. 55

III, m. 167

Allegro vivace

Beethoven

83. Faust, Act I, no. 6

Tempo di valzer

Gounod

Like the gentle breeze . . .

84. H.M.S. Pinafore, "I'm Called Little Buttercup"

Sullivan

10. Submediant and Mediant Triads

Questions for Analysis

1. How are the submediant and mediant triads introduced and resolved? Which chord tone is doubled?
2. Where do sequences occur? Analyze in detail.

---

85. Herzliebster Jesu, was hast du verbrochen

Crüger

86. Dir, dir, Jehovah, will ich singen

Anon.

87. Schmücke dich, o liebe Seele

Bach

88. Bastien und Bastienne, K. 46B, no. 1
m. 11

Andante, un poco adagio

Mozart

Mein lieb-ster Freund hat mich ver-las-sen, mit ihm ist Schlaf und

Ruh' da-hin, mit ihm ist Schlaf und Ruh' da-hin.

My dear friend has forsaken me, sleep and rest have left with him.

89. Sonata, K. 545

Mozart

Rondo

90. Sonata in F for Flute and Continuo
II

Allegro

Handel

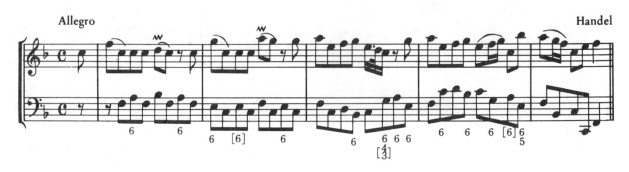

91. Rigoletto, Act I, no. 1

Allegro con brio

Verdi

92. Symphony No. 4, op. 98
IV

Allegro giocoso

Brahms

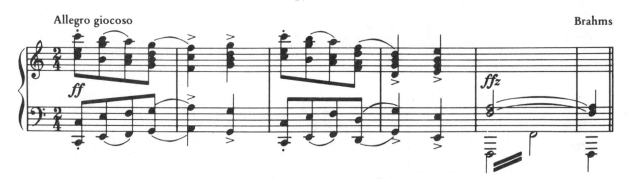

93. Sonata for Violin and Continuo, op. 5, no. 9
II, m. 5

94. Quartet in D major, D. 74

*This implies V7/IV.

95. Trio, op. 1, no. 3

Beethoven

96. Sonata, K. 283

Mozart

97. Menuet

J. C. F. Bach

vii°7

---

98. Au joli bois je m'en vais

Tessier

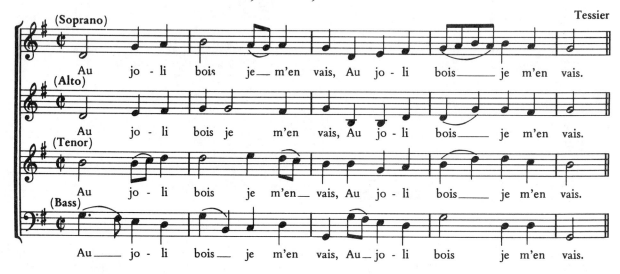

(Soprano)
Au   jo - li   bois   je — m'en   vais,   Au   jo - li   bois ____ je   m'en   vais.

(Alto)
Au   jo - li   bois   je   m'en   vais,   Au   jo - li   bois ____ je   m'en   vais.

(Tenor)
Au   jo - li   bois   je   m'en — vais,   Au   jo - li   bois ____ je   m'en   vais.

(Bass)
Au ____ jo - li   bois — je   m'en   vais,   Au — jo - li   bois   je   m'en   vais.

To the pretty woods I go.

---

99. Der Rosenkavalier, Act III
Reh. 297, m. 3

Strauss

p (Sophie)
Ist   ein   Traum,   kann   nicht   wirk - lich   sein, ____

p (Octavian)
Spür'   nur   dich,   spür'   nur   dich,   al - lein ____

Ruhig gehend   ♩=69

pp

Sophie: It is a dream, it can't really be true that we two are together for all time
  and eternity.
Octavian: Know that I love only you and that we two are together. Everything
  passes before my sight as a dream.

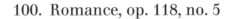

100. Romance, op. 118, no. 5

101. Phantasiestücke, op. 12, no. 4: Grillen
m. 17

Mit humor

Schumann

102. Im Abendroth (Posthumous)

Langsam, feierlich

Schubert

con Ped.

O, wie schön ist dei - ne Welt, Va - ter, wenn sie gol - den

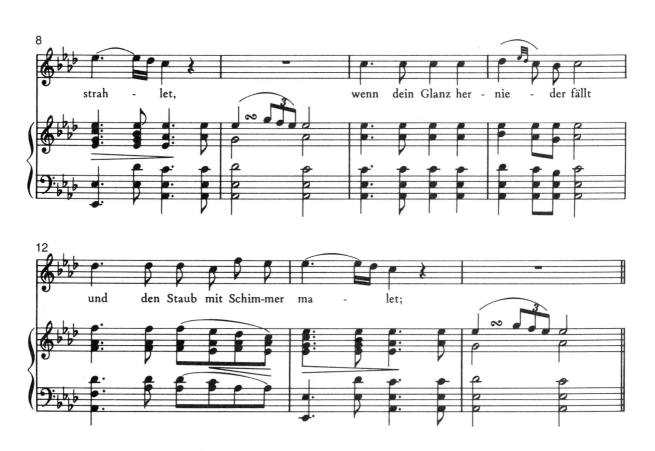

strah - let, wenn dein Glanz her - nie - der fällt

und den Staub mit Schim-mer ma - let;

O, how beautiful is Thy world, Father, when it shines like gold, when Thy brightness falls upon it and paints the dust with shimmering brightness.

103. Symphony in C major ("The Great")

Andante

Schubert

*Refer also to Unit 11.

11. Leading Tone Triad

Questions for Analysis

1. How is the leading tone triad introduced and resolved?
2. Where do cadences occur? How are they established? Do phrases form periods? Of what type?

104. Schatz über alle Schätze

Teschner

105. Aus meines Herzens Grunde

Bach

106. Album for the Young, op. 68: Soldatenmarsch

m. 25

Schumann

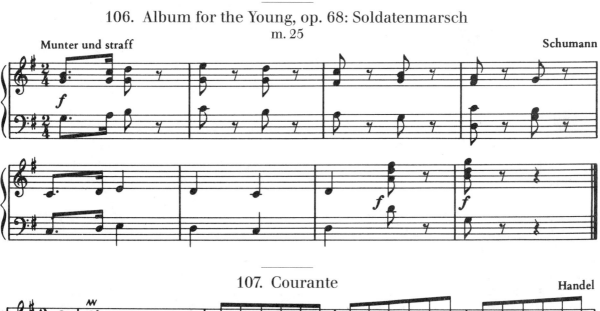

107. Courante

Handel

108. Sonata in E♭ major, Hob. XVI: 49

I

Haydn

109. Sonatina in D major, Hob. XVI: 4

I

Haydn

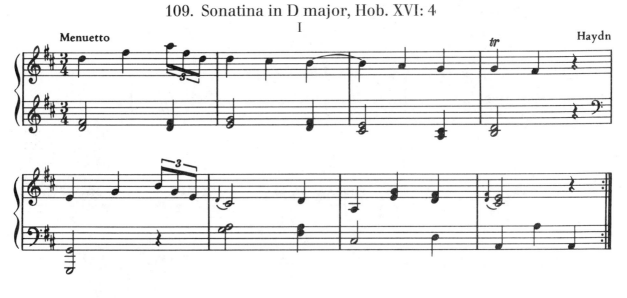

110. Sonata, K. 280
I, m. 131

Allegro assai

Mozart

111. La Joyeuse

12. Variant Qualities of Diatonic Triads

Questions for Analysis
1. Identify all scalar variants and modally borrowed chords.
2. Carefully analyze the qualities of all chords in this unit.

SCALAR VARIANTS IN MINOR

___

112. Herr, ich habe mißgehandelt

Bach

113. Chaconne

Pachelbel

114. Fantasie No. 8

Telemann

Vivace

---

115. Pavana "The Earle of Salisbury"

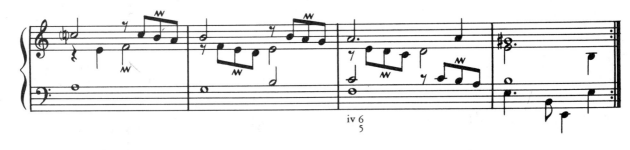

iv 6
5

---

116. Folia

---

117. Minuet

Matteson

---

118. Sonata, K. 310
III, m. 211

Mozart

119. La Traviata, Act I, no. 4
m. 16

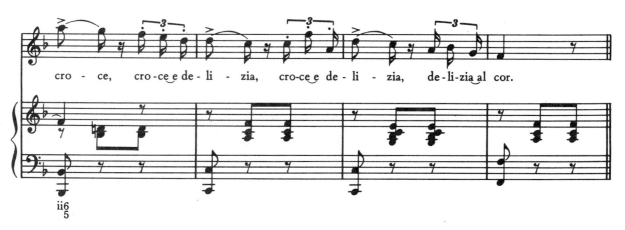

croce,   cro-ce e de-li - zia,   cro-ce e de-li - zia,   de-li-zia al cor.

ii6
5

Love, which is the moving force of the entire universe,
The mysterious one, the proud one, the cross and delight to the heart.

120. Linda di Chamounix, "O Luce di quest' anima"

Allegretto

Donizetti

6

Oh, light of this soul, delight and love and life, our fate will be united on earth and in heaven.

121. Sonata for Violin and Piano, K. 306
m. 51

Mozart

122. Sonatina in C major, Hob. XVI: 7
III, m. 26

Allegro

Haydn

123. Aufenthalt

Schubert

Non troppo vivace, con fuoco

Rau - schen - der Strom,   brau - sen - der Wald,   star - ren - der

Fels, mein Auf - ent - halt; rau - schen - der Strom,

V^6_5/iv

brau - sen - der Wald, star - ren - der Fels, mein Auf - ent - halt.

Rushing stream, blustering wood, immobile rocks, my abode.

124. Der Wanderer
m. 32

Etwas geschwinder

Schubert

Wo bist du, wo bist du, mein ge - lieb - tes

Land? ge - sucht, ge - ahnt,

Where are you, my beloved country? Sought for, yearned for, and never known!

---

125. Symphony No. 3, op. 90
II, m. 128

126. Il Trovatore, Act II, no. 11
m. 50

Verdi

V7/ii

Azucena: Plunge this blade up to the hilt into the heart of the cruel one. Strike!
Manrico: Yes, I swear it. This blade will descend into the heart of the cruel one.

127. Symphony No. 5, op. 67
III, m. 27

Beethoven

128. Symphony No. 4, op. 98
II

Andante moderato

Brahms

13. Supertonic Seventh Chord

Questions for Analysis

1. How is the seventh of the ii7 introduced and resolved?
2. Where do cadences occur? Do phrases form periods?

129. Herr, wie du willst, so schick's mit mir

Anon.

130. Straf' mich nicht in deinem Zorn
I

Bach

131. Sonata in A♭ major, Hob. XVI: 46
III

Presto

Haydn

13. SUPERTONIC SEVENTH CHORD   81

132. Voegtersang

Molto andante e semplice

Grieg

133. Symphony No. 6, op. 68
V, m. 237

Allegretto

Beethoven

134. Quartet, op. 168, D. 112
III

MENUETTO
Allegro

Schubert

135. Sonata, K. 310
I, m. 129

Allegro maestoso

Mozart

136. Ständchen

Schubert

Lei - se fle - hen mei - ne Lie - der durch die Nacht zu dir;

My songs float lightly through the night to you.

137. Symphony No. 2, op. 36
II, m. 246

138. Sonata, op. 14, no. 2
I

139. Symphony No. 6, op. 68
III, m. 53

Beethoven

140. Carmen, Act II: Entr'acte

Allegro moderato

Bizet

141. Blue Moon

Slowly, with feeling

Rodgers

Blue Moon!_____ Now I'm no long-er a-lone___

With - out a dream in my heart,___

With - out a love of my own

14. Leading Tone Seventh Chord

Questions for Analysis

1. What is the quality of the leading tone seventh chord in each example? Is the chord diatonic or altered?
2. How is the seventh introduced and resolved?
3. Where do cadences occur? How are they established?

142. Quartet, op. 96
m. 156

Dvorak

143. Sonata, K. 457

Mozart

144. Carnaval, op. 9: Chiarina

Schumann

145. Ballade, op. 10, no. 4
m. 89

Andante con moto

Brahms

146. Sonata for Flute and Continuo

Handel

Larghetto

147. Allegro

Haydn (?)

148. Trio in G major, Hob. XV: 25

m. 121

Haydn

149. Requiem, K. 626: Offertorium

Lord Jesus Christ, King of Glory! Free the souls of all the faithful from death's bonds.

150. Sonatina in G major, Hob. XVI: 11
III, m. 44

Haydn

151. Judas Maccabaeus, Part III: no. 53, Introduction

152. Das Rheingold, Scene 1

Allmanlich etwas Langsamer

Wagner

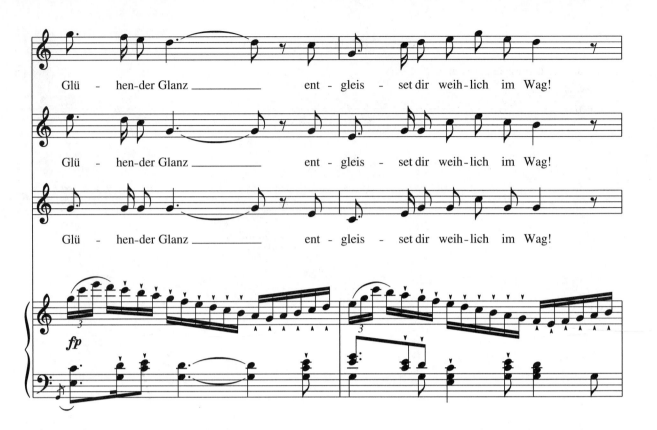

Rhine gold! Rhine gold!
Bright joy!
How you laugh, so clear and majestic
Glowing luster, you glisten daringly.

153. Orphée, Act I, no. 1
m. 15

Gluck

si ton om - bre nous en - tend,

si ton om - bre nous en - tend,

si ton om - bre nous en - tend,

si ton om - bre nous en - tend,

vii°7/V

Ah, in this dark and quiet wood, Euridice, if thy spirit hears us . . .

154. Aria con Variazioni, Leçon No. 1
II

Handel

155. Fantasia, 1er Dozzina, no. 5
II

Grave   Telemann

156. Sonata for Violin and Piano, K. 306

15. Other Diatonic Seventh Chords

Questions for Analysis

1. How are the chord sevenths introduced and resolved?
2. Where do sequences occur? Analyze both harmonically and melodically (motivically).
3. Discuss the texture of all the examples. Which are predominately homophonic and which predominately polyphonic?

---

157. O Ewigkeit, du Donnerwort

Bach

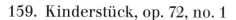

---

158. Rondo, K. 494
m. 95

Andante

Mozart

---

159. Kinderstück, op. 72, no. 1

Allegro moderato

Mendelssohn

160. Fantasie

Pachelbel

161. Sonata for Flute and Continuo

Allegro

Handel

162. Leçon No. 2, Menuet

Handel

163. Symphony No. 4, op. 36
II

Tchaikovsky

Andantino in modo di canzona

p   semplice ma grazioso

164. French Suite in D minor

16. Complete Pieces for Analysis I

Checklist for Analysis

✓ *Subjective aspects, including affect, mood, expression:* How are these achieved?

✓ *Stylistic aspects:* What features of the music tell us who wrote it?

✓ *Form:* Overall form, cadences, phases, periodic structure if any.

✓ *Rhythm:* Meter, rhythmic patterns (motives), special effects. How is continuity achieved, and where are the resting points?

✓ *Harmony:* Harmonic details, including cadences, chords, inversions, nonharmonic tones. Which are the structural chords? Which are embellishing or linear?

✓ *Line:* Structural pitches, motives, cadence figures; placement of climax, if any.

✓ *Counterpoint and voice-leading:* How do the outer voices relate to each other in terms of intervals, intervallic patterns, relative motion, and so on? Are all tendency tones conventionally resolved?

✓ *All aspects of pattern:* Accompaniment patterns, harmonic and motivic patterns; patterns of nonharmonic tones.

165. Minuet

166. Dance

Schubert

167. German Dance, op. 33, no. 12

Schubert

168. Scottish Dance

Beethoven

169. Rigadoon

Purcell

170. Minuet

Rameau

vii°⁷/V

171. Passacaglia

Witt

*Additional variations follow.

172. Norsk

Presto marcato

Grieg

II. Chromatic Materials

Suggestions for Discussion

This section introduces the chromatic vocabulary (secondary dominants and other altered chords) and techniques of modulation. As with the previous section, it is essential that your analysis go beyond mere labeling of key and chords. Particularly with the modulating examples, consider the way in which the first key is established and the devices by which the composer effects the modulation to the new key. All aspects of formal design must be considered, including motive, figuration pattern, phrase, period, cadence, and harmonic rhythm. Be attentive to such details as sequence, repetition, and contrapuntal relationships.

Additional Aspects to Consider

- All instances of chromaticism in a line: Are they functional (chord members) or nonharmonic; are they used sequentially and/or motivically?
- All chromatically altered chords: Are they functional or linear; what diatonic chords do they replace; what sequential or other patterns do they form? Where are they used within the piece?
- Again, we direct your attention to the *Suggestions for Using This Book* on page xxi and reiterate the importance of *hearing* the music in class and of discussing *all* the musical elements and their interactions.

17. Secondary (Applied, Borrowed) Dominants

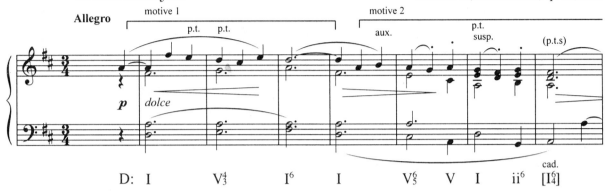

Model Analysis   Beethoven, *Piano Sonata, op. 10, No.3*

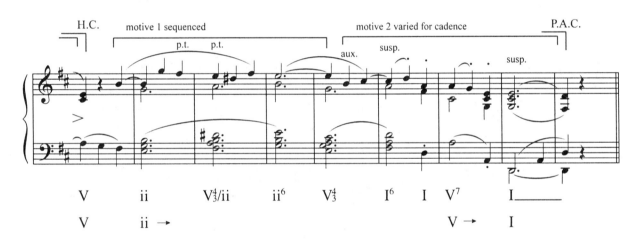

Observations:

A. Form: two eight-measure phrases, H.C. P.A.C. a | a', forming a sequential period. The underlying structural harmony supports the two-section parallel structure.

B. The harmonic rhythm is quite regular: one chord per measure, except speeding up approaching the first cadence. As noted above, the underlying structural harmony is very simple:

$$ I \quad \overset{\text{H.C.}}{V} \quad ii \quad \overset{\text{P.A.C.}}{V \quad I} $$

C. There appear to be two motivic gestures, a rising idea and a falling one (building and then releasing tension through shape of line). The melodic line (mm. 1-3) is supported by a rising bass line, both treated sequentially in the second phrase (mm. 9-11). Study the bass line in terms of the harmonic implications of its scale degrees.

D. The structural upper voice and bass lines are somewhat complex in this excerpt. You may wish to make a linear reduction of both.

E. See also Appendix A, page 503.

Questions for Analysis

1. How are secondary dominants introduced? Which are the tendency tones and how are they resolved?
2. Where do cadences occur? Analyze each as to type.

173. Trio, op. 1, no. 1

Beethoven

174. Sonata, K. 281

III

175. Impromptu, op. 142, no. 3

Schubert

176. Trio in D major
I, m. 178

Haydn

177. Sonatina in G major
II

Beethoven

178. Oberon: Overture
m. 65

Allegro con fuoco

Weber

179. Trio, op. 1, no. 1

180. Sonata, op. 118ᶜ, Andante

Ausdrucksvoll

Schumann

181. Symphony No. 1, op. 21

Adagio molto

Beethoven

182. Suite XI

Sarabande

Handel

183. Arabeske, op. 18

Leicht und zart

Schumann

184. Symphony No. 4, op. 60

185. Widmung, op. 25, no. 1

Schumann

Grab, in das hin - ab ich e - wig mei - ne Kum - mer gab!

Thou my soul, Thou my heart, Thou my joy, oh Thou my pain, Thou my world
in which I live; Thou my Heaven, where in I soar; so Thou my grave, in which
I bury my grief forever.

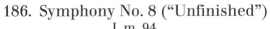

186. Symphony No. 8 ("Unfinished")
I, m. 94

Schubert

Allegro moderato

187. Sonata, op. 118ᶜ, Puppenwiegenlied
III, m. 9

Schumann

Nicht schnell

188. Quintet ("Die Forelle"), op. 114, D. 667
III, m. 93

Schubert

189. Quintet, op. 29

Beethoven

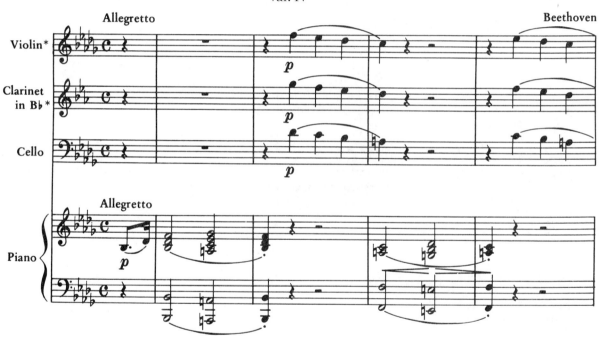

190. Trio, op. 11
Var. IV

*May be performed with either violin or clarinet.

---

191. Rigoletto, Act II, no. 7
m. 194

Verdi

In heaven, close to God, a protective angel watches. Ah, watch over this flower.

192. Suite XVI

Courante   Handel

193. Sonata, op. 53
I, m. 34

Allegro con brio   Beethoven

194. Symphony in C major ("The Great")
II, m. 93

Andante con moto   Schubert

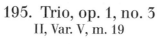

195. Trio, op. 1, no. 3
II, Var. V, m. 19

196. Mass in E♭ major: Benedictus

Schubert

9

ne - di - ctus qui ve - nit in no - mi - ne Do - mi - ni,

ne - di - ctus qui ve - nit in no - mi - ne Do - mi - ni,

Be - ne -

Blessed is he who cometh in the name of the Lord.

197. Midsummer Night's Dream, op. 61: Wedding March

Allegro vivace

Mendelssohn

198. Rigoletto, Act II, no. 14
m. 64

Pardon will come to us from Heaven. This clown knows how to strike you down.

199. Christmas Oratorio, no. 4: Introduction

200. Sonata VII for Flute and Continuo
II

201. Mazurka, op. 67, no. 2
m. 17

202. Valse, op. 69, no. 1

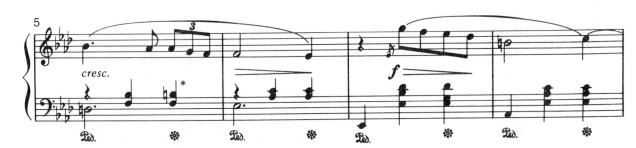

*See Part II, Unit 20.

203. Valse Brillante, op. 34, no. 3
m. 54

Chopin

*See Part II, Unit 20.

204. Someone to Watch Over Me

Gershwin

205. Morning Prayer

Andante

Tchaikovsky

206. Can I Forget You?

Kern

18. Modulation to Closely Related Keys

Questions for Analysis

1. Where and by what means do the modulations occur?
2. Is the new key confirmed after the point of modulation; if so, how?
3. What is the overall form of each example?

MODULATION TO DOMINANT

207. Symphony No. 39, K. 543

ALLA TURCA

208. Sonata, K. 331

209. Symphony No. 2, op. 36
III

Beethoven

210. Minuet

Haydn

211. Quartet, D. 173
IV

Allegro

Schubert

7

212. Sonata in C♯ minor, Hob. XVI: 36
II

Allegro con brio

Haydn

6

213. Symphony No. 41, K. 551
III

214. Mazurka, op. 7, no. 2

Chopin

Vivo, ma non troppo

215. Sonata in G major, Hob. XVI: 39

III

Allegro

Haydn

216. Sonata, K. 282, Menuet I

217. Quartet, D. 173
II

Andantino   Schubert

218. Trio in F♯ minor, Hob. XV: 26
II

219. Sonata in E minor, Hob. XVI: 34
III

Molto vivace

Haydn

220. Sonata, K. 330
II, m. 21

Andante cantabile

Mozart

221. Lucia di Lammermoor, Act I, Cavatina

Reigning in the silence was the darkening night. The forehead was
struck by a pallid ray of the gloomy moon.

222. Quintet, op. 115

223. Symphony No. 7, op. 92

Beethoven

224. Symphony No. 104, Hob. I: 104

Haydn

N₆

225. Sonatina, Hob. XVI: 1
II, m. 21

Haydn

226. Deh più a me non vàscondete

Bononcini

Con sve - lar - vi, se voi

sie - te, voi po - te - te far que - st'al - ma fuor di duol, voi po -

te - te far que-st'al-ma — fuor di duol, ——— far que'st'al-ma — fuor di — duol.

By unveiling yourselves (if you are about to do that) you can take this soul out of pain.

227. Carneval des Animaux: Le Cygne

228. Waltz, op. 39, no. 15 228

Brahms

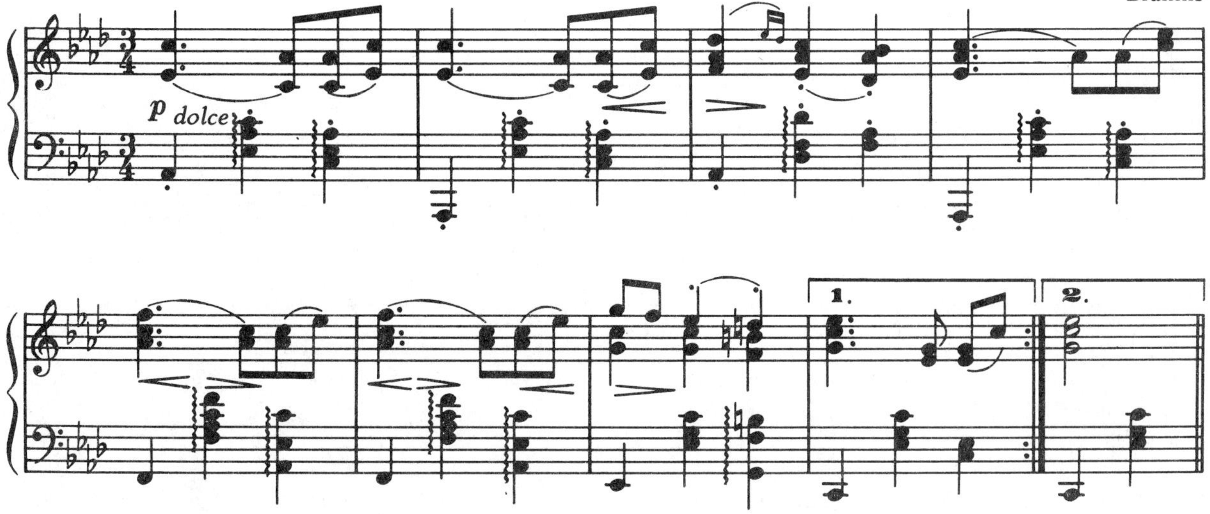

229. Quartet, op. 18, no. 2 229

IV

Allegro molto quasi presto

Beethoven

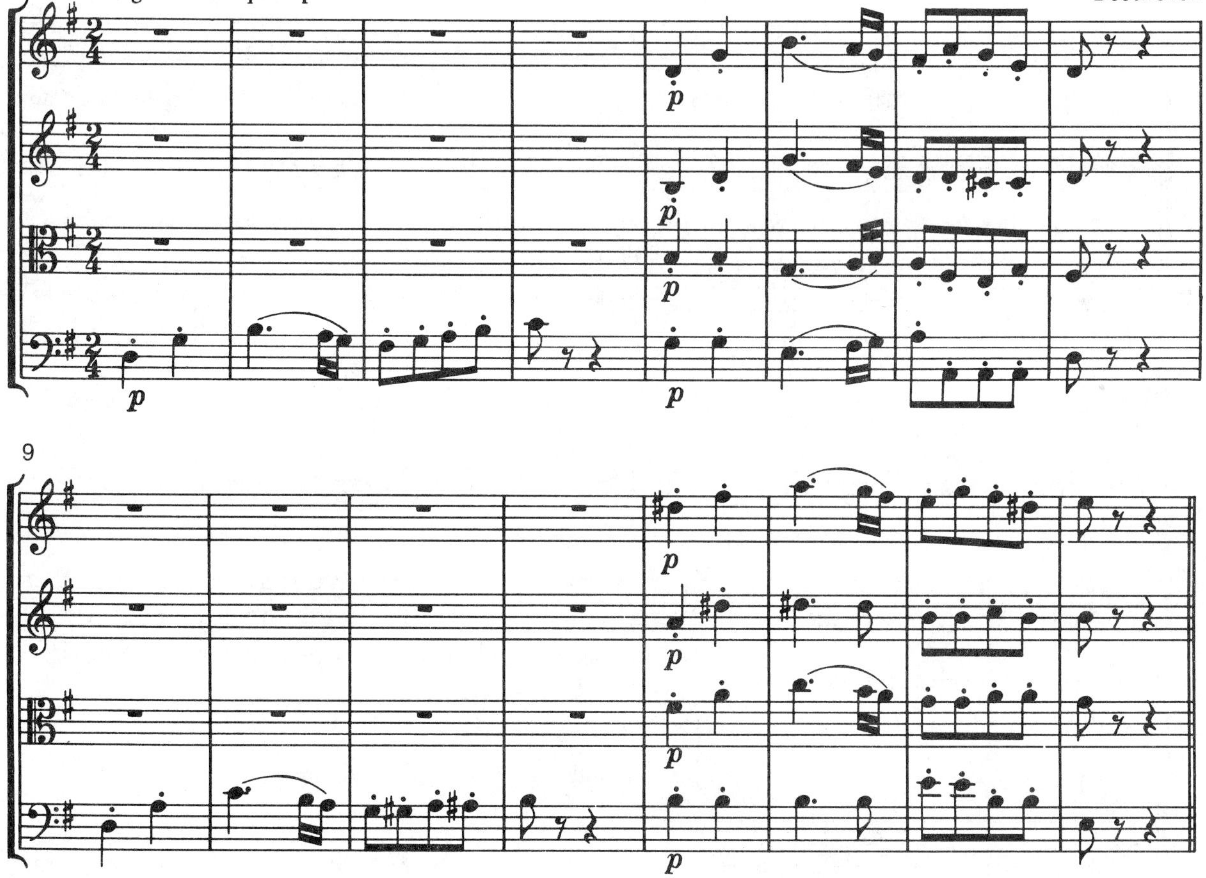

230. Dido and Aeneas, Act I, scene I
Reh. 4, m. 19

Purcell

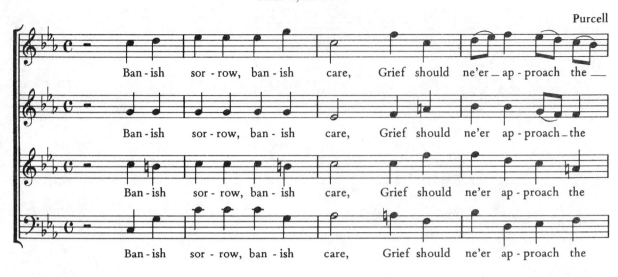

Ban-ish sor-row, ban-ish care, Grief should ne'er ap-proach the

Ban-ish sor-row, ban-ish care, Grief should ne'er ap-proach the

Ban-ish sor-row, ban-ish care, Grief should ne'er ap-proach the

Ban-ish sor-row, ban-ish care, Grief should ne'er ap-proach the

fair, Ban-ish sor-row, ban-ish care, Grief should ne'er ap-proach, should ne'er ap -

fair, Ban-ish, ban-ish, care, ban-ish sor-row, Grief should ne'er, should ne'er ap -

fair, Ban-ish sor-row, ban-ish, ban-ish care, Grief should ne'er ap-proach, should ne'er ap -

fair, Ban-ish sor-row, ban-ish, ban-ish care, Grief should ne'er ap -

proach the fair, grief should ne'er ap-proach the fair.

proach the fair, grief should ne'er, should ne'er ap-proach the fair.

proach the fair, grief should ne'er, should ne'er ap-proach the fair.

proach the fair, grief should ne'er ap-proach the fair.

231. French Suite in C minor

Bach

19. Complete Pieces for Analysis II

Checklist for Analysis

✓ *Subjective aspects, including affect, mood, expression:* How are these achieved?

✓ *Stylistic aspects:* What features of the music tell us who wrote it?

✓ *Form:* Overall form, cadences, phases, periodic structure if any.

✓ *Rhythm:* Meter, rhythmic patterns (motives), special effects. How is continuity achieved, and where are the resting points?

✓ *Harmony:* Harmonic details, including cadences, chords, inversions, nonharmonic tones. Which are the structural chords? Which are embellishing or linear?

✓ *Line:* Structural pitches, motives, cadence figures; placement of climax, if any.

✓ *Counterpoint and voice-leading:* How do the outer voices relate to each other in terms of intervals, intervallic patterns, relative motion, and so on? Are all tendency tones conventionally resolved?

✓ *All aspects of pattern:* Accompaniment patterns, harmonic and motivic patterns; patterns of nonharmonic tones.

---

232. Wachet auf, ruft uns die Stimme

Bach

233. In dulci jubilo

Bach

234. Christ lag in Todesbanden

Bach

235. Menuet

Handel

236. Sonata, op. 26
II

Beethoven

237. Sonata, op. 118ᵇ, Abendlied

238. Waltz, op. 39

Brahms

239. Prelude

Allegro

Handel

240. Sonatina in F major

Allegro assai

Beethoven

241. Sonata in G major, Hob. XVI: 27

Haydn

Menuet da Capo

---

242. You Took Advantage of Me

Rodgers

Refrain (liltingly)

I'm a sen - ti - men - tal sap, that's all.___ What's the use of try - ing

p a tempo

*

not to fall?___ I have no will,___ You've made your kill___ 'Cause you

*See Unit 20.

*See Unit 23.

20. Linear (Embellishing) Diminished Seventh Chords

Questions for Analysis

1. Which chords are clearly functional? Which are linear?
2. What combinations of nonharmonic tones create the linear chords?

---

243. Symphony No. 104, Hob. I: 104, Menuet

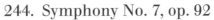

---

244. Symphony No. 7, op. 92
III, m. 149

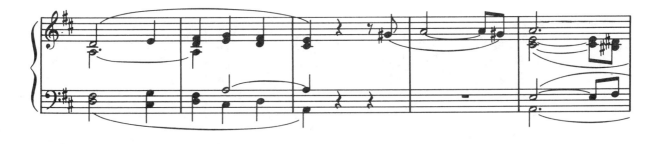

245. Les Préludes
m. 260

Liszt

246. Contradanse

Beethoven

247. Symphony No. 6, op. 74
I, m. 90

Andante

Tchaikovsky

20. LINEAR (EMBELLISHING) DIMINISHED SEVENTH CHORDS   183

248. Quartet, op. 18, no. 3
II

Andante con moto

Beethoven

7

249. Sonata, op. 53
II

Con moto
legato

Schubert

250. Faust, Act IV, no. 18
m. 204

Faust: Sweet nectar, let my heart be enshrouded in your rapture, while a kiss of fire caresses my pale brow until daybreak.

251. Carnaval, op. 9: Arlequin
m. 17

Schumann

252. Waltz, K. 567

Mozart

253. Rienzi: Overture

254. I Puritani, Act II, scene 3
Reh. 24, m. 23

Here his sweet voice was calling for me and then it disappeared. Here he was swearing to be faithful, and then the cruel one escaped from me.

---

255. Symphony No. 104, Hob. I: 104

II

Haydn

256. The Girl Friend

Refrain (a little faster and rhythmical)

Rodgers

Is - n't she cute! Is - n't she sweet! She's

gen - tle and men - tal - ly near - ly com - plete. She's

knock - out, she's re - gal, her beau - ty's il - le - gal, She's the

girl friend!

257. Liebeslieder Walzer, op. 52, no. 4

Brahms

I wish to glow to you like the beautiful red of the evening, to please one person, to spread delight without end.

21. Neapolitan Triad

Questions for Analysis

1. How is the Neapolitan triad introduced and resolved?
2. Where does the Neapolitan triad occur within the phrase? Is the chord in root position or inversion? Is it tonicized or used in a modulation?

258. Concerto in A major, K. 488
II

259. Der Müller und der Bach

Wo ein treu - es Her - ze in Lie - be ver - geht, da

Where a true heart pines away for love, there droop the lilies on every bank.
Clouds conceal the moon so that men may not see her tears. Angels close their
eyes, and cry and sing the soul to rest.

260. Ach Gott, vom Himmel sieh' darein

Bach

261. Invention No. 13
m. 18

Bach

262. Il Trovatore, Act II, no. 8
m. 35

che ____ s'al za al ciel!

Sinister shines on the terrible faces the gloomy flame that rises to the sky.

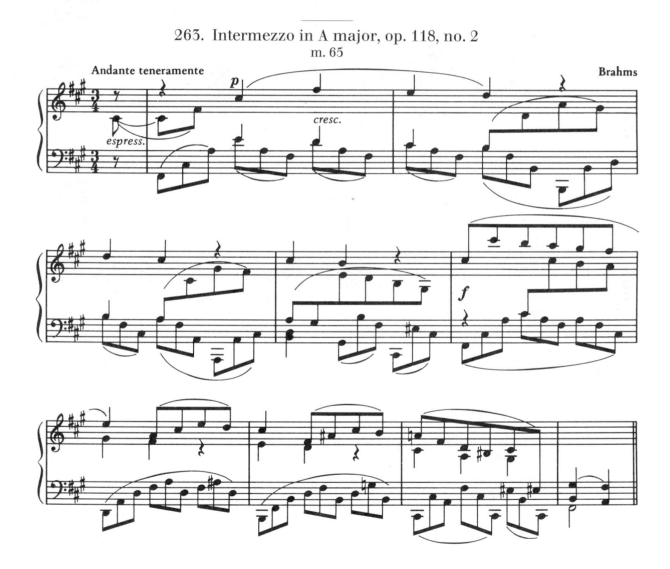

263. Intermezzo in A major, op. 118, no. 2
m. 65

Andante teneramente   Brahms

264. Prelude, op. 28, no. 20

Chopin

265. String Quartet, op. 59, no. 2
I

Allegro

Beethoven

266. Wie Melodien zieht es mir, op. 105

Zart

Brahms

Wie Me - lo - di - en ____ zieht es mir lei - se durch den

Sinn, wie Früh - lings-blu - men blüht es und schwebt wie Duft da - hin.

As melodies drift lightly through my senses, as spring flowers bloom and their
fragrance floats away.

267. Quartet, op. 18, no. 3
III

Allegro

Beethoven

268. Mass in E♭ major: Credo

Schubert

I believe in one God, maker of heaven and earth.

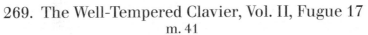

269. The Well-Tempered Clavier, Vol. II, Fugue 17
m. 41

Bach

---

270. Prelude, op. 28, no. 6

22. Augmented Sixth Chords, Submediant Degree as Lowest Note

Questions for Analysis

1. Where do augmented sixth chords occur?
2. How are these chords introduced and resolved?
3. Where do cadences occur? How are they established?

ITALIAN

271. Ich hab' mein' Sach' Gott heimgestellt

Bach

272. Bagatelle, op. 119, no. 1
m. 9

Beethoven

273. Coriolan Overture, op. 62

Allegro con brio

Beethoven

---

274. Mazurka

Tempo di mazurka

Tchaikovsky

---

275. Quartet, op. 168, D. 112

IV

Presto

Schubert

276. Symphony No. 1, op. 21
II, m. 65

Beethoven

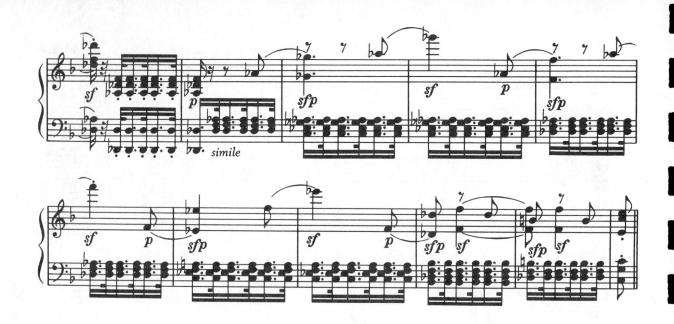

GERMAN

277. Sonata, K. 457
III, m. 167

278. Sonata, op. 109
III

Andante molto cantabile ed espressivo

mezza voce

Beethoven

279. Trio, Hob. XV: 25

Haydn

280. Thirty-Two Variations, Var. 30

Sostenuto

Beethoven

281. Chanson Sans Paroles, op. 40, no. 2

Andantino

Sibelius

282. Der Rosenkavalier, Act I
Reh. 233

Strauss

Having armed my heart with vigor against love, I rebelled. But I was defeated in a flash, alas! by looking at two delicate rays.

FRENCH

283. Elijah, op. 70, no. 1

Mendelssohn

284. Mass in G major: Kyrie
m. 30

Christ, have mercy upon us.

285. Wer nur den lieben Gott läßt walten

Bach

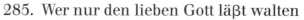

286. Sonata, op. 42
I

Schubert

287. La Traviata, Act III: Prelude

288. Symphony in C major ("The Great")
II, m. 8

289. Alfedans, op. 12
m. 9

Grieg

290. Gypsy Love Song

Herbert

291. Dichterliebe, op. 48, no. 12: "Am leuchtenden Sommermorgen"

On a brightening summer morning, I go into the garden. The flowers whisper and speak, but I wander silently.

23. Augmented Sixth Chords, Other Scale Degrees as Lowest Note

Questions for Analysis

1. How are the augmented sixth chords introduced and resolved?
2. Where do cadences occur? How are they established?

292. Adagio

Mozart (?)

293. Valses Poeticos

Moderato

Granados

294. Symphony No. 8 ("Unfinished")
II

Schubert

295. Songs and Dances of Death, no. 4

Moussorgsky

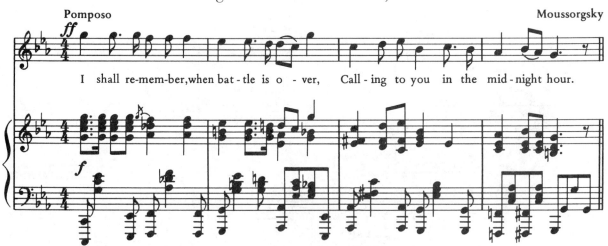

Posposo

I shall re-mem-ber, when bat-tle is o - ver, Call-ing to you in the mid-night hour.

296. Orphée, Act I, nos. 6 and 7

Gluck

Object of my love . . .

24. Augmented Sixth Chords, Other Uses

Question for Analysis

1. How do the arrangement of the chord and the voice-leading serve to establish the particular usage of the chord?

LINEAR

297. Rigoletto, Act I: Prelude

Verdi

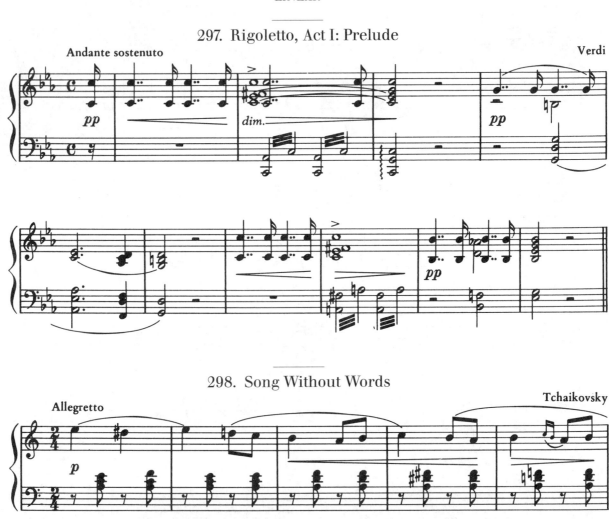

298. Song Without Words

Tchaikovsky

299. Romeo and Juliet
m. 251

300. Waltz

Schubert

301. Intermezzo, op. 76, no. 4

Allegretto grazioso

Brahms

302. The Witch

303. Prelude, op. 28, no. 22

304. Mass in G major: Benedictus

Be - ne - di - - - ctus qui

Blessed is he who cometh in the name of the Lord.

305. Die Allmacht, op. 79, no. 2

Schubert

Great is Jehovah the Lord, for heaven and earth proclaim His power.

306. Quintet, op. 163
IV, m. 417

Schubert

307. Liebestraum, no. 3

Liszt

Poco allegro, con affetto

308. Snowmaiden: Chanson du Bonhomme Hiver

Rimsky-Korsakov

Poco animato

6

309. Solvejg's Lied
m. 8

25. Other Means of Modulation

Question for Analysis

1. Identify the initial key and the key(s) to which the examples modulate. What modulatory devices are employed?

---

310. Mass in G major: Gloria
m. 40

Soprano: Lord God, Lamb of God.
Bass: Son of God, who taketh away the sins of the world.
Chorus: Have mercy upon us.

311. Wenn du nur zuweilen lächelst, op. 57, no. 2

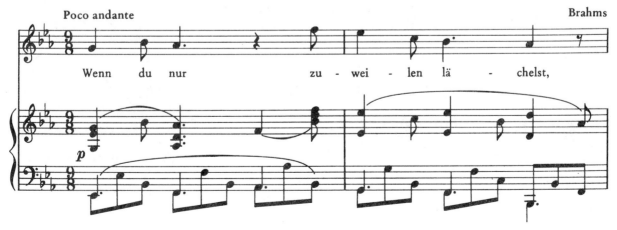

nur___ zu - wei - len Küh - le fä - chelst

die - ser un - ge-mess - nen Glut, die - ser un - ge - mess - - nen Glut.

If you would only occasionally smile, or occasionally cool my boundless ardor . . .

312. Symphony No. 5, op. 67
II, m. 23

Beethoven

313. Waltz, op. 9, no. 14, D. 365
m. 17

Schubert

314. Die Entführung aus dem Serail, K. 384, Act III, no. 18

Allegretto

Mozart

6 Pedrillo

In Moh - ren - land ge - fan - gen war_____ ein

In Moorishland, a pretty maiden with black hair was imprisoned. She wept day
and night and would gladly have been rescued.

315. Symphony No. 2, op. 61
III

Schumann

316. Symphony No. 7, op. 92
II, m. 117

Beethoven

317. String Quartet, op. 76, no. 6
III, m. 31

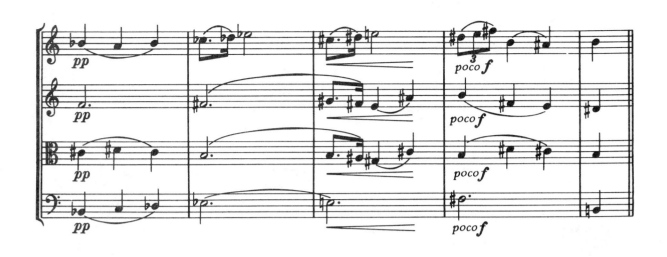

318. Sonata, op. 13
I, m. 132

Beethoven

319. Trio, op. 70, no. 1
IV, m. 375

Beethoven

320. Prelude, op. 13, no. 3

Scriabin

321. Dic Fledermaus: Overture
Reh. 3, m. 29

J. Strauss

322. Wie bist du meine Königin, op. 32, no. 9
m. 39

Brahms

Through dead wastes I wander, green shadows broadening about me, endlessly
onward through the frightful oppressiveness, pleasureful . . .

323. Mass in A♭ major: Agnus Dei

Lamb of God, who taketh away the sins of the world, have mercy upon us.

324. Trio, op. 11
II, m. 27

*Violin and clarinet are alternate parts.

325. Melodie, op. 3, no. 3
m. 10

Adagio sostenuto

Rachmaninoff

326. Symphony No. 8 ("Unfinished")
II, m. 64

Schubert

26. Ninth Chords

Questions for Analysis

1. How is the ninth introduced and resolved?
2. Is it clearly heard as a chord tone, or in some cases might it better be analyzed as nonharmonic?
3. Is the chord complete or incomplete? If incomplete, which notes are missing?
4. Discuss the texture of each example.

DOMINANT NINTHS

327. Artist's Life Waltzes, op. 316, no. 3
m. 17

J. Strauss

328. Sonata for Violin and Piano
I

Allegretto ben moderato

Franck

329. Andante

Beethoven

330. Valse Brillante, op. 34, no. 1
m. 128

Chopin

331. Waldesgespräch, op. 39, no. 3

Ziemlich rasch

Schumann

Es ist schon spät,＿ es ist schon kalt,＿ was
reit'st du ein-sam durch den Wald? Der wald＿ ist lang, du bist＿ al-
lein, du schö-ne Braut, ich füh'r dich heim,

It is late, it is cold, why do you ride alone through the woods? The way is long,
you are alone—lovely bride, I will lead you home.

---

332. Prelude, op. 28, no. 15

Chopin

Sostenuto

333. St. Matthew Passion, no. 78

Bach

334. Genoveva, op. 81: Overture

Schumann

335. Grandmother's Minuet, op. 68, no. 2

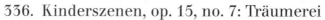

336. Kinderszenen, op. 15, no. 7: Träumerei

NONDOMINANT NINTHS

337. Wedding Day at Troldhaugen, op. 65, no. 6

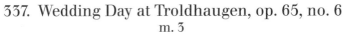

m. 3

Tempo di marcia

Grieg

338. Midsummer Night's Dream, op. 21: Overture
m. 450

339. Après un Rêve
m. 17

You called me and I left the earth to fly with you toward the light. The skies half
opened their clouds to us, partially revealing unknown splendors, divine lights . . .

27. Extended Linear Usages

Questions for Analysis

1. Which chords are clearly functional and which are linear?
2. Are there chords that could be analyzed as either linear or functional?
3. How does voice-leading create linear chords?

---

340. Mazurka, op. 6, no. 1

Chopin

341. "Der Tod, das ist die kühle Nacht," op. 96, no. 1

Brahms

Death, it is the cool night; life, the sultry day.
It grows dark, I become sleepy; the day has made me tired.

342. Euryanthe: Overture
m. 129

Weber

343. Variations on a Theme by Handel, var. 20

Brahms

344. Symphony in D minor
III, m. 318

Allegro non troppo

Franck

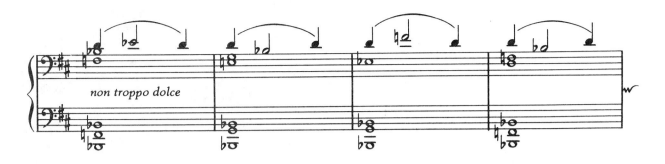

non troppo dolce

---

345. Lohengrin, Act I, scene 2
m. 118

Allmählich noch etwas langsamer

Wagner

346. Wotan's Farewell, Die Walküre, Act III
m. 624

Wagner

347. Lover

Refrain (very vivaciously and spiritedly)

Rodgers

Lov - er,_____ when I'm near you_____ And I hear you_____

_____ speak my name_____ Soft - ly_____ in my

ear you_____ breathe a flame._____

348. Prelude, op. 28, no. 9

349. Quartet, op. 18, no. 6

LA MALINCONIA
Questo pezzo si deve trattare colla più gran delicatezza.

Beethoven

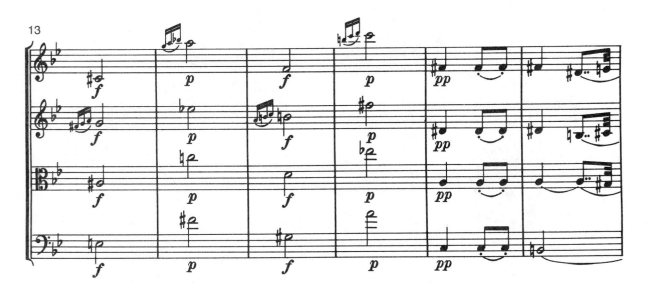

28. Complete Pieces for Analysis III

Checklist for Analysis

✓ *Subjective aspects, including affect, mood, expression:* How are these achieved?

✓ *Stylistic aspects:* What features of the music tell us who wrote it?

✓ *Form:* Overall form, cadences, phases, periodic structure if any.

✓ *Rhythm:* Meter, rhythmic patterns (motives), special effects. How is continuity achieved, and where are the resting points?

✓ *Harmony:* Harmonic details, including cadences, chords, inversions, nonharmonic tones. Which are the structural chords? Which are embellishing or linear?

✓ *Line:* Structural pitches, motives, cadence figures; placement of climax, if any.

✓ *Counterpoint and voice-leading:* How do the outer voices relate to each other in terms of intervals, intervallic patterns, relative motion, and so on? Are all tendency tones conventionally resolved?

✓ *All aspects of pattern:* Accompaniment patterns, harmonic and motivic patterns; patterns of nonharmonic tones.

350. Minuet, K. 355

351. Myrthen, op. 25, no. 24

Schumann

14

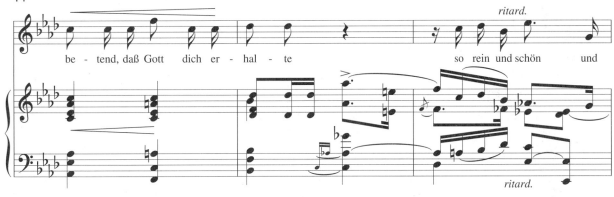

be - tend, daß Gott dich er - hal - te   so rein und schön   und

ritard.

17

hold.

ritard.

You are like a flower, just as charming, beautiful and pure; I look at you, and sadness steals into my heart. It seems to me I should place my hands on your head, praying that God keep you so pure, beautiful, and charming.

---

352. Lieder ohne Wörte, op. 30, no. 3

Adagio non troppo   Mendelssohn

353. Mazurka, Op. posth. 67, no.2

Chopin

354. Phantasiestücke, op. 12, no. 3: Warum?

Schumann

355. Erotikon

Grieg

356. Il pensieroso, from Années de Pèlerinage

Liszt

357. Morgen, op. 27, no. 4

R. Strauss

And tomorrow the sun will shine again, and on the way where I am going, we,
the happy ones, will again be one in the midst of the sun-drenched earth. And
toward that far and hazy horizon, we will quietly and slowly wander. Mute, we
will gaze into each other's eyes, while on us falls the blissful silence.

358. Der Engel

führt er, fer - ne je - dem Schmerz, mei - nen Geist nun

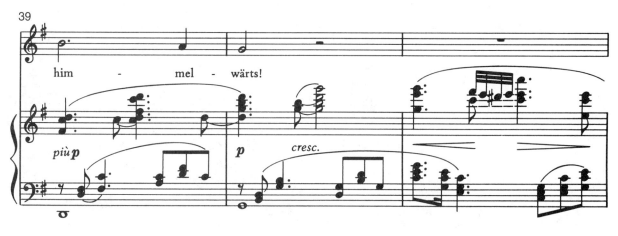

him - mel - wärts!

In the early days of childhood, I often heard about angels who exchange the joys of heaven for earth's sunshine; so that wherever a sorrowful heart, hidden from the world, pines; wherever it bleeds silently and fades away in tears; wherever its earnest prayer begs for release; there the angel sweeps down and gently carries it to heaven. Yes, an angel also came down to me, and on shining wings, far from all pain, bears my soul to heaven!

359. Sieben Variationen:
Über das Volkslied: "God Save the King"

Beethoven

Var. III

Var. IV

360. Symphony No. 40, K. 550
III

Trio 43

49

55

D.C. Menuetto

361. Phantoms

Beach

362. A Breeze from Alabama: March and Two-Step

Joplin

363. Smoke Gets in Your Eyes

Kern

364. Sonata, K. 309

Allegro con spirito

Mozart

Allegretto grazioso

29. Examples of Counterpoint

Questions for Analysis

In this unit, in addition to the musical aspects you have been investigating, the following are also to be noted:

1. *Voice function and importance:* Are the voices equal and self-contained as lines? Do they have both independence and interdependence? Is there any feeling that one voice is ever supportive or accompanimental?

2. *Line:* Is each voice clearly shaped and motivically coherent? What are the melodic idioms at cadential points? Is melodic material shared between the voices?

3. *Harmony:* Is the harmony clear and functional? Are nonharmonic tones used consistently within the style? Is the harmonic rhythm steady? Are there any linear harmonies?

4. *Rhythm:* Is the meter clearly established and maintained? Are there rhythmic motives? Is there any sense of rhythmic growth through the phrase?

5. *Counterpoint:* What harmonic (vertical) intervals do you find on all beats and on the strongest beats? Are all dissonances and tendency tones resolved? What durational (rhythmic) ratios do you find between or among the voices? What directional relationships?

6. *Imitation:* Where there is imitation, what are the pitch interval and rhythmic interval between the entering voices? How long does the imitation continue?

7. *Sequence:* Are there sequences? How are they transposed? Are all voices involved? How many times are they repeated?

8. *Special techniques:* Are there any, such as stretto, melodic inversion, diminution, retrogression, or pedal point?

---

365. Ein' feste Burg ist unser Gott

Bach

366. Es ist genug, so nimm, Herr

Bach

367. Cantata No. 4: Sinfonia

Bach

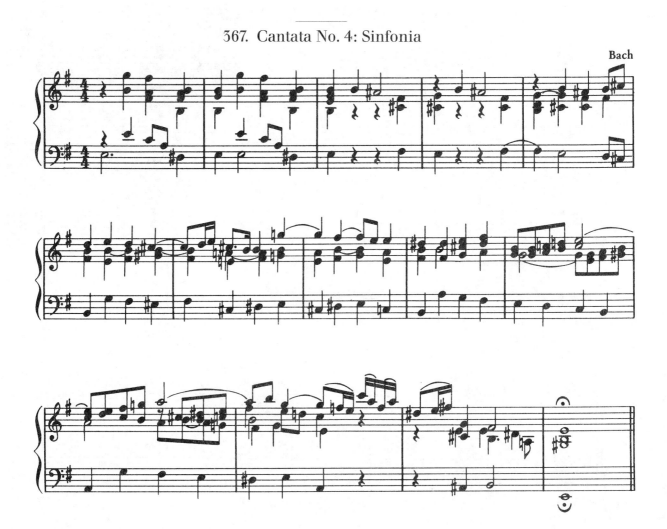

368. Chorale Prelude on "In Dulci Jubilo"*

Bach

*The chorale on which this prelude is based may be found in Unit 19, no. 233.

369. Chorale Prelude on "Christ lag in Todesbanden"*

Bach

*The chorale on which this prelude is based may be found in Unit 19, no. 234.

370

370. Chorale Prelude on "O wie selig seid ihr doch, ihr Frommen"

371. "Thy Hand Belinda", from *Dido and Aenas*

Purcell

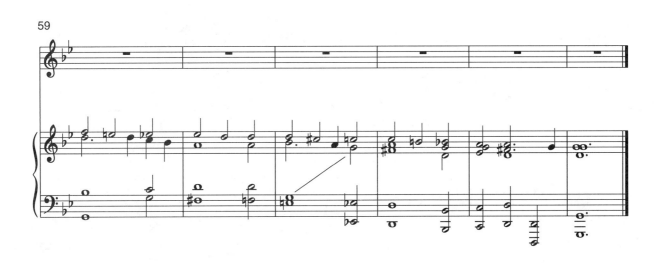

59

372. Invention No. 4, BWV 775

Bach

5

10

15

373. Invention No. 13, BWV 775

Bach

374. Sinfonia 3, BWV 789

Bach

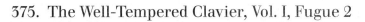

375. The Well-Tempered Clavier, Vol. I, Fugue 2

376. The Well-Tempered Clavier, Vol. II, Fugue 9

Bach

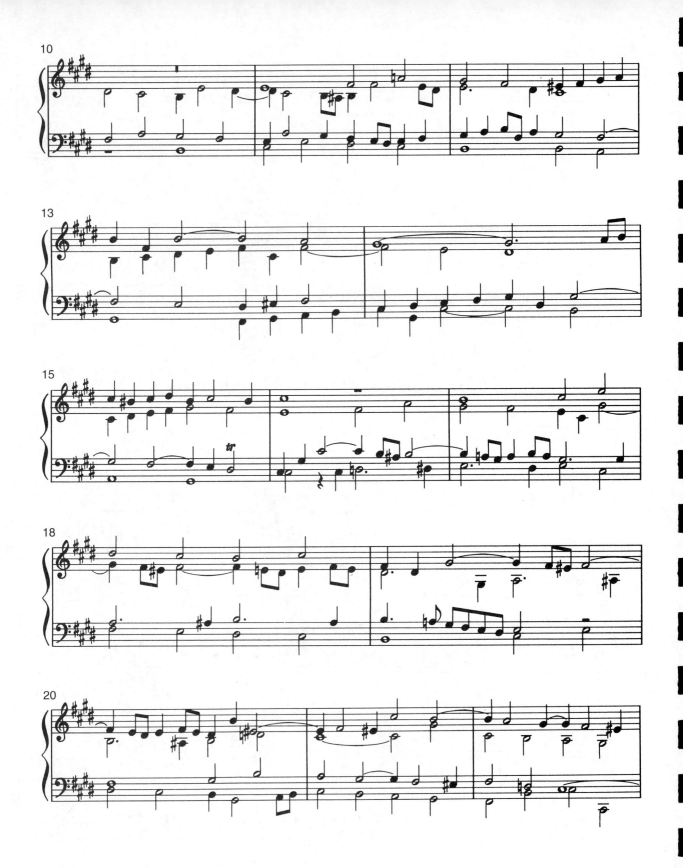

---

377. Fugue No. 2, op. 35

Tranquillo e sempre legato

Mendelsshon

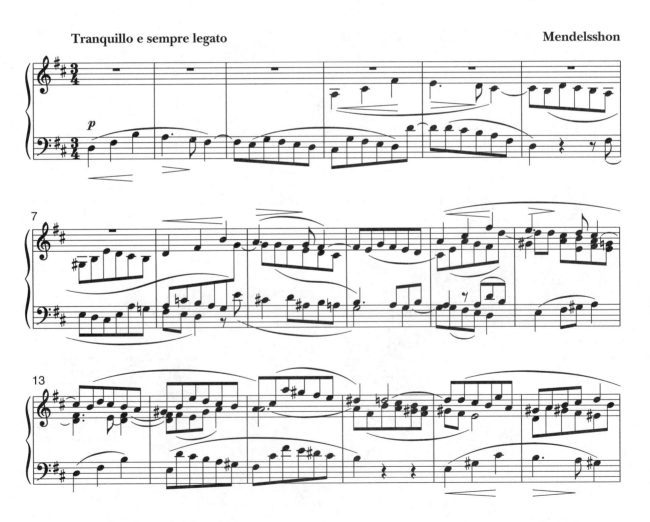

Additional Examples for the Study of Contrapuntual Techniques

III. Contemporary Materials

Suggestions for Discussion

Much of the music in this section can be heard and understood as an extension of common practice music, not necessarily requiring radically new methods of analysis. The underlying principles that unify older musics are still operative in this music, to a greater or lesser extent: traditional formal structures, cadences, regular phrase structures, and even at times periodic structure, motivic and gestural content, well-shaped melodies, rhythmic patterning and metric regularity, highly logical and consistent pitch organization, clear tonal centers, and so on. In many examples, the only nontraditional aspect is that of pitch relationships; in every other way much of this music is not very different in aesthetic or technique from that of the preceding several centuries.

At the same time, some new analytical approaches may be useful in understanding this music. With this in mind, each unit is prefaced by a few questions meant to guide your discussions and to suggest appropriate avenues of inquiry. These questions are by no means exhaustive, and many others will occur to you.

Additional Aspects to Consider

- Is there a tonal center, or centers, and how are they achieved (by line and harmony)? Do they change, and if so by what means?
- What formal structures are used—statement, departure, return; cadence and phrase structure; repetition, varied repetition, contrast, development?
- How are the pitches chosen? Is there a traditional or other scale or mode in use, and if so which? Is the scalar/harmonic material an extension of traditional tonal materials? Is the pitch organization purely intervallic? Is there a serial organization?
- What are the means of coherence—motivic, rhythmic, textural, registral, color, dynamic?
- How is the harmony structured? How are chords constructed (of what intervals)? How is their succession determined (any patterns)?
- How do counterpoint and voice leading play a role?
- Rhythm: Is the meter clear, and if so how is it made so? Are there any special effects (polyrhythm, polymeter, ametrical effects, isorhythmic patterns)?
- Be sure, as always, to discuss aspects of style, interrelation of the musical elements, and performance issues.

We would like again to direct your attention to the *Suggestions for Using This Book* on page xxi and to reiterate the importance of *hearing* the music in class and of discussing *all* the musical elements and their interactions.

30. Extended and Altered Tertian Harmony

Questions for Analysis

1. Does functional (roman numeral) analysis apply to any of these excerpts? Are keys and chord structures clear and in traditional relationships? Are some other pitch descriptive systems more useful here, such as jazz/pop chord symbols?
2. In what other ways are these excerpts similar to common practice music? Consider form, phrase structure, motive, theme, counterpoint, and so on.
3. In what ways do they represent departures from older techniques?

---

378. Symphony No. 2, op. 30
I, reh. F

Hanson

---

379. Sonatina, op. 13

Kabalevsky

380. Mysterious Mountain
I, m. 12

Andante con moto

Hovhaness

381. Prelude, op. 34, no. 24

Shostakovich

382. Pelléas et Mélisande, Act I, scene 1
m. 178

Debussy

383. Poem, op. 32, no. 2

Allegro; con eleganza; con fiducia

Scriabin

384. Valses Nobles et Sentimentales
m. 53

Ravel

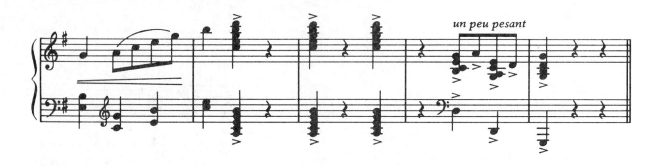

385. Slaughter on Tenth Avenue

Junior dances with Vera's dead body.

Andante doloroso

Rodgers

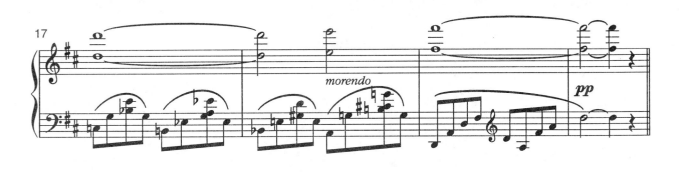

386. September Song

387. Prelude to a Kiss

Ellington

Moderato

How my love song gen - tly cries___ for the ten - der - ness with -

in your eyes___ My love is a pre - lude that nev - er dies___

A PRE - LUDE TO___ A KISS.___

mf

388. Jordu

Med. Up Jazz — Duke Jordan

389. Four Songs, op. 2, no. 3

Berg

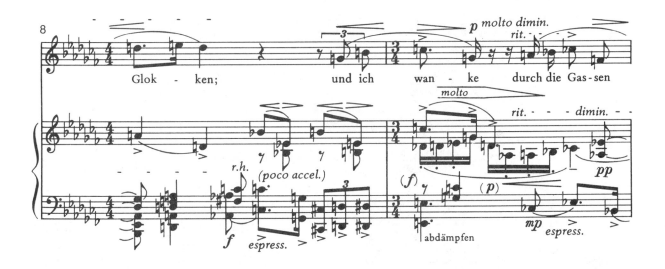

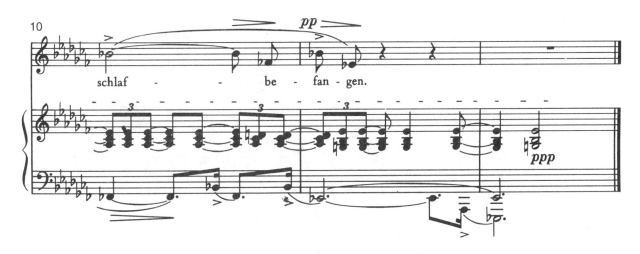

Now that I have defeated the strongest of giants, have found my way home from the darkest land on a white fairy-tale hand, the bells sound heavily and I stagger through the alleys, caught in sleep.

31. Diatonic (Church) Modes

Questions for Analysis

1. By what means are the tonal center and mode made clear?
2. Are there instances of mixing, layering, or shifting of modes within any excerpt?
3. What sorts of harmonic structures are present? Are they always clearly tertian?

---

390. Little Pieces for Children, no. III

391. Ten Preludes, no. 1

392. Valse

393. Trois Chansons, no. 1

Très modéré, soutenu et expressif

Debussy

Dieu! qu'il la fait bon re - gar - der La gra - ci - eu - se bonne et

bel - le;

God! He has made her attractive, gracious, good, and beautiful.

394. Toccatina

Allegretto

Kabalevsky

7

31. DIATONIC (CHURCH) MODES 379

395. Ceremony of Carols, no. 8

396. Suite bergamasque: Passepied

Debussy

Allegretto ma non troppo

397. Susannah, Act II, scene 3

Susannah   Floyd

Andante piangendo (♪=96)

trees on the moun-tains are cold___ and bare. The sum - mer jes' va - nished an'

left___ them there like a false - heart - ed lov - er jes' like ___ my own who

made me love_him, then left_me a - lone.

398. Five Fingers: Lento

Stravinsky

399. Fourteen Bagatelles, op. 6, no. 4

Bartok

400. Siciliana

Allegretto dolcemente mosso

(il ritmo sempre molto preciso)

Casella

p espressivo, semplice, come una melodia popolare

pp dolcissimo

401. Work Song

Adderley

32. Pandiatonicism and Additive Harmony

Questions for Analysis

1. Is Roman numeral analysis applicable to any of these excerpts? What other systems of harmonic description might also be helpful? Are all these excerpts essentially tertian?
2. What scales and/or modes do you find? By what means are scale and mode made clear?
3. What elements distinguish this music from common practice music using the same materials?

---

402. Mother Goose Suite: The Magic Garden

403. Touches Blanches

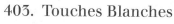

404. The Irishman Dances

405. The Young Pioneers
m. 32

Copland

406. Excursions, III
m. 49

Barber

407. Petroushka: Danse Russe

Stravinsky

408. Gloria: Laudamus te

We praise thee.

33. Exotic (Artificial, Synthetic) Scales

Questions for Analysis

1. How are tonal center and scale made clear?
2. What are the interval characteristics of each scale? What intervals are missing from any given scale? What effect does this have on the music? What analytic systems (Hanson, Persichetti, interval vector) might be useful in understanding this music?
3. Is there any shifting, mixing, or changing of scales within any excerpt?

409. Touches Noires

409

410. Mikrokosmos, no. 78: Five Tone Scale

410

411. Valsette

Kodály

412. London Symphony
I, Reh. M

Vaughan Williams

413. Préludes, II: Voiles

Modéré (♪=88)
(Dans un rythme sans rigueur et caressant.)

Debussy

414. Mikrokosmos, no. 136: Whole Tone Scale

Andante, ♩ = 108

Bartok

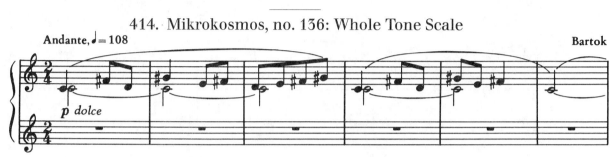

415. Pelléas et Mélisande, Act II, scene 1
m. 137

Lento

Debussy

416. Fourteen Bagatelles, op. 6, no. 10
m. 10

Bartok

417. Bucolic, no. 3
m. 20

Lutoslawski

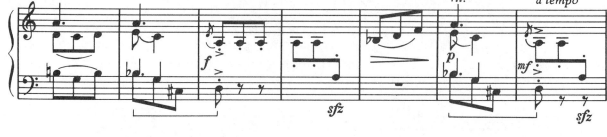

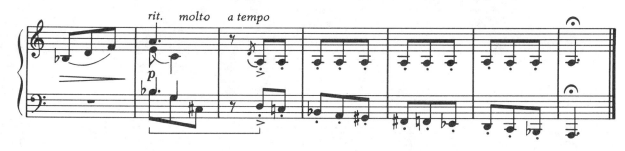

418. Mikrokosmos, no. 101: Diminished Fifth

Bartok

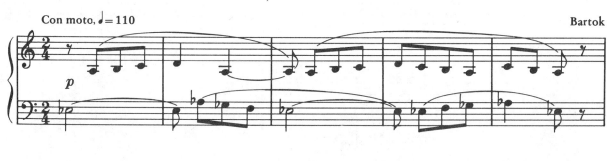

Con moto, ♩ = 110

p

6

419. Sketches, op. 9, no. 6

Bartok

420. Fourteen Bagatelles, op. 6, no. 6

Bartok

34. Quartal and Secundal Harmony

Questions for Analysis

1. What sorts of interval structures are used to organize each excerpt? How consistent are they within each? Does each have a clear tonal center and if so, how is it emphasized?
2. What new analytic systems would be applicable to this music? Consider pitch and interval class analysis, Hanson, Persichetti, and perhaps others.
3. What are the traditional and nontraditional elements in each excerpt? Make lists of both aspects.

---

421. Mathis der Maler: Grablegung

Hindemith

---

422. Majority
m. 20

Ives

The Mas - ses are think - ing, Whence comes the thought of the

World!

423. Piano Piece, op. 39, no. 5

Krenek

424. Ludus Tonalis, Fuga secunda in G

425. Concerto for Orchestra
I, m. 316

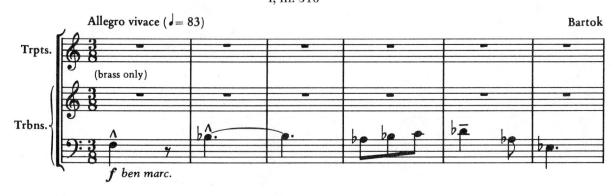

426. Wozzeck, Act II

Langsam (♩.=56-60) aber nicht schleppend

Berg

Mä - del, was fangst Du jetzt an? _____ Hast ein klein Kind und kein

Mann! _____ Ei, was frag' ich dar - nach, _____

Sing' _____ ich die gan - ze Nacht.

"Maiden, what are you doing now? You have a small child and no husband.
Oh, what are you asking for?" I sing the whole night through.

427. Mikrokosmos, no. 107: Melody in the Mist

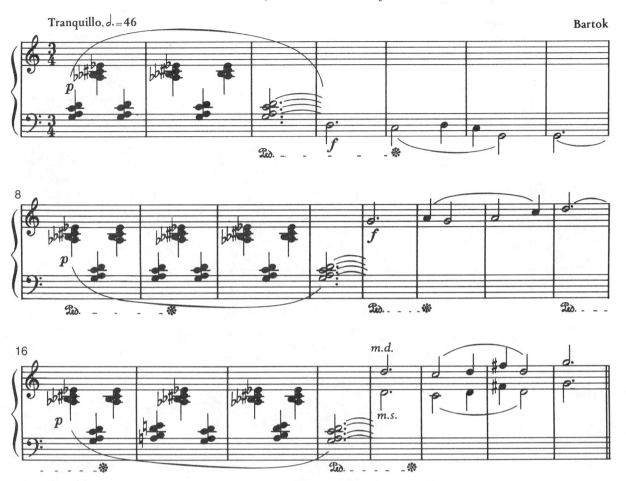

Tranquillo, ♩.=46

Bartok

428. Wozzeck, Act II

A hunter from the palace once rode through a green wood.

429. Tiger

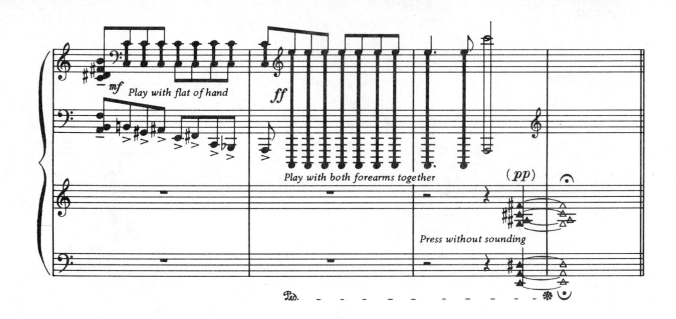

Play with flat of hand
Play with both forearms together
Press without sounding

---

430. Majority

Slowly

Ives

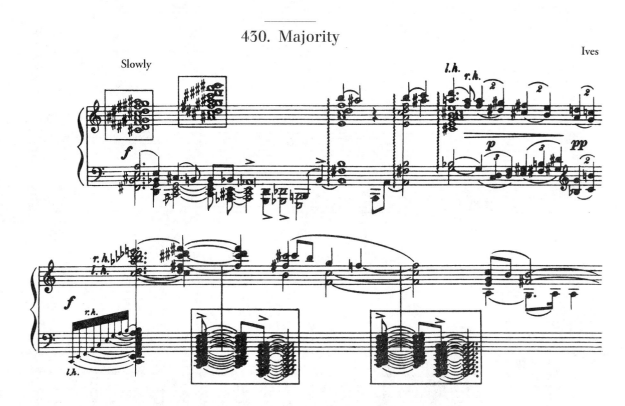

431. Blue Rondo à la Turk
m. 57

Lively ♩.= 126 (♪= 378)

Brubeck

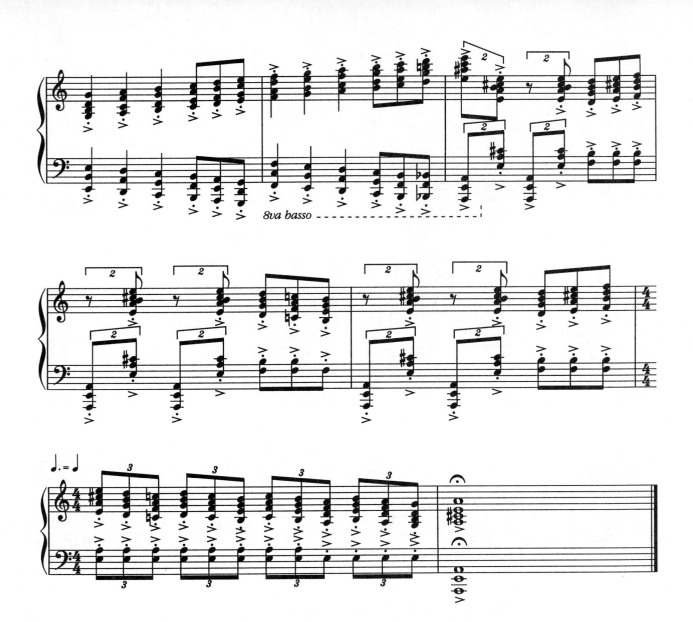

35. Polyharmony and Polytonality

Questions for Analysis

1. Which examples are polyharmonic? Which are polytonal? Which are both?
2. What is the nature of the harmonic structures? Do they combine traditional chords or not? What root relationships between keys or chords do you find? Are they systematically worked out?
3. Are tonal centers clear? How are they emphasized? What scale systems are used? Does any example *not* use a traditional scale?

---

432. Symphony No. 5
I

---

433. A Three-Score Set, II

434. Allegro Giocoso
m. 31

Kraft

435. The Rake's Progress: Prelude

Stravinsky

436. Petroushka, Scene 2
Reh. 95, m. 9

Stravinsky

437. Saudades do Brazil, no. 7: Corcovado
m. 19

438. Forty-Four Violin Duets, no. 33

439. Strange Meadowlark
m. 37

Brubeck

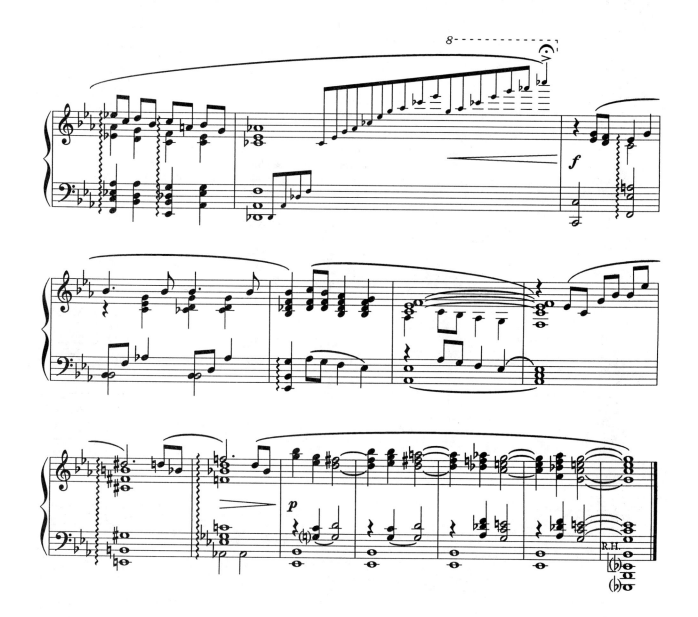

36. Free Atonality

Questions for Analysis

1. This sort of music is often referred to as "atonal," but are there perceptible tonal centers in any of these excerpts? If so, how are these established?
2. Which intervallic "cells" or sets are used to unify each example? To what extent do these seem consistent? Which intervals in each seem important? Which less so? Apply set-theoretic (pitch- and interval-class and interval vector) analysis.
3. What are the other means of unification? Consider theme, gesture, motive, phrase structure, register, rhythm, and so on.

---

440. Drei Klavierstücke, op. 11, no. 1

441. Klavierstücke, op. 19, no. 2

442. Pierrot Lunaire, op. 21, no. 1: Mondestrunken

Schönberg

The wine one drinks with one's eyes
Pours down nightly in waves from the moon.
And a spring-tide flood washes over
The silent horizon.

443. Five Movements for String Quartet, op. 5, no. 4

Webern

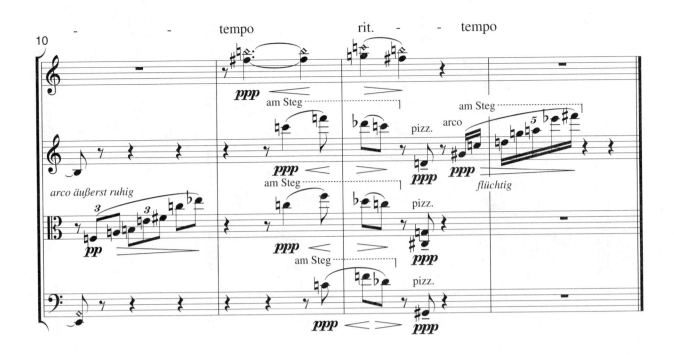

444. Mikrokosmos, no. 144: Minor Seconds, Major Sevenths

445. Fourth String Quartet

I

Bartok

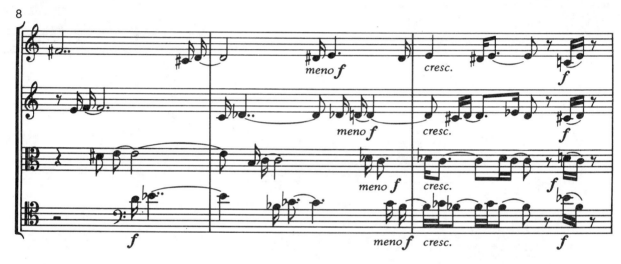

446. From My Diary, III

Sessions

447. Two Episodes, I

Berger

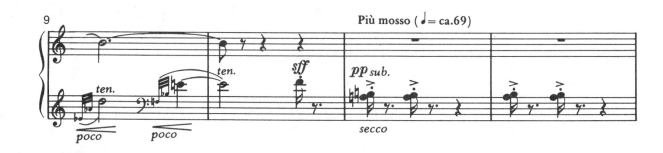

37. Twelve-Tone Serialism

Questions for Analysis

1. For each excerpt, label each row-form at its beginning, using whatever system your instructor suggests; number each note in the row. Write down each row (in terms of pitch-class integers or letter names) or construct a magic square (matrix), if your instructor so requests. What are the interval characteristics of each row? What melodic and harmonic intervals are emphasized in the music? Is the row always consistently and fully used? Are the pitches always in order? Does a statement of the row coincide with some sort of structural articulation, such as a phrase or motivic statement?

2. Where different row-forms are used in the same piece, successively or simultaneously, why are these particular forms (and not others) used? Consider such issues as pitch-class invariants, segmentation of rows, and combinatoriality.

3. Aside from the serial aspects, what traditional organizing elements are found in each excerpt? Consider form, phrase, theme, motive, rhythm, gesture, meter, and so on.

448. Dancing Toys, op. 83, no. 1

Allegretto moderato ♪= 120

Krenek

449. Suite für Klavier, op. 25: Gavotte

Etwas langsam ($\quad$ = ca.72) nicht hastig

Schönberg

450. Cinque Frammenti di Saffo

Full shone the moon, when by the altar they stopped. And the Cretian woman, with music, upon light feet, began carefree to go about the altar, upon the tender young grass.

451. Drei Lieder, op. 25, no. 1

How happy I am! Once again everything becomes green and glowing to me!
Still the flowers bloom over all my world! Once again I have been placed
entirely in becoming and am on the earth.

38. Music Since 1945*

Questions for Analysis

1. Listen carefully and repeatedly to the assigned examples. What elements of pitch organization are present? What other aspects of unification are used?
2. In what ways are the nonpitch aspects of any given example important? Consider texture, color, register, rhythmic activity (attack and sustain density), dynamics, and so on.
3. What nontraditional ways of performing and of listening are called for in these excerpts?

---

452. Klavierstücke, no. 2

Stockhausen

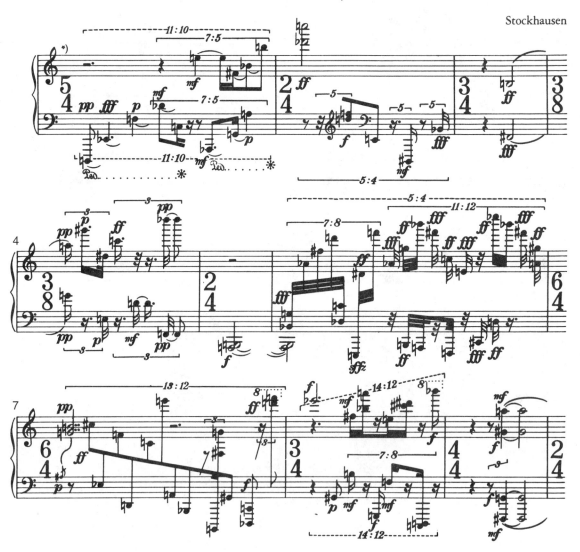

*For explanation of new notational procedures, see complete scores of the pieces included in this unit and *Music Notation in the Twentieth Century* by Kurt Stone (New York: W. W. Norton, 1980).

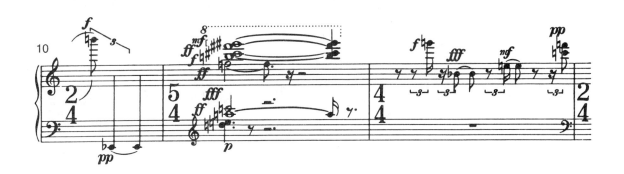

---

453. String Quartet (1965)
m. 33

Lutoslawski

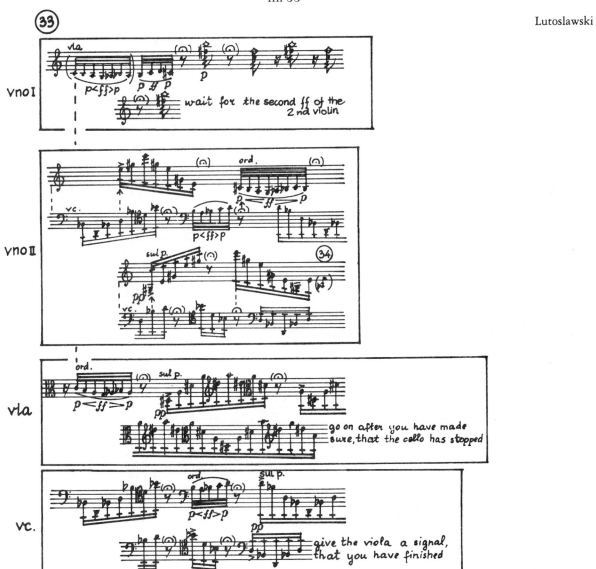

454. String Quartet, no. 2

Vivace

Penderecki

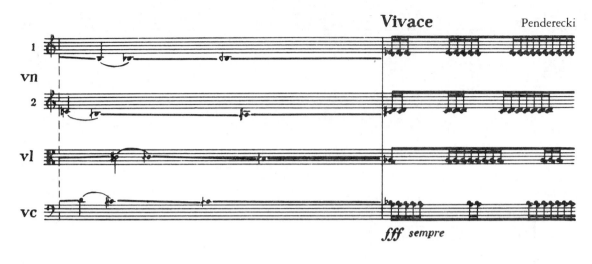

fff sempre

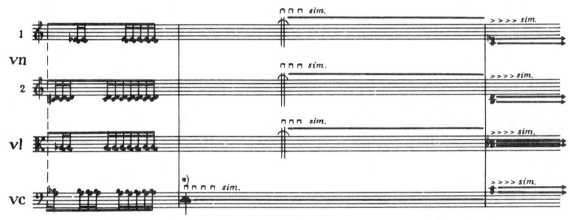

*) mit dem Bogen auf der rechten Schmalseite des Steges spielen
bow the right narrow side of the bridge

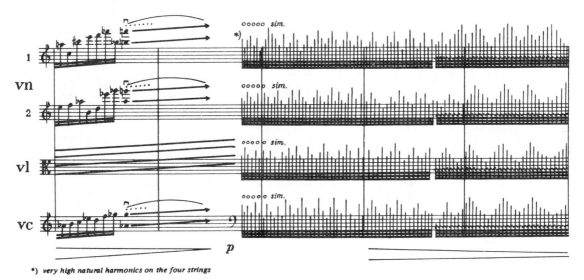

*) very high natural harmonics on the four strings

Lento molto

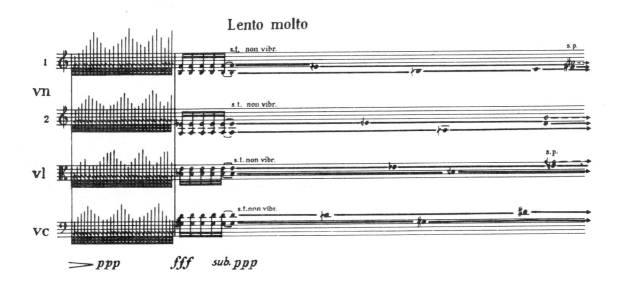

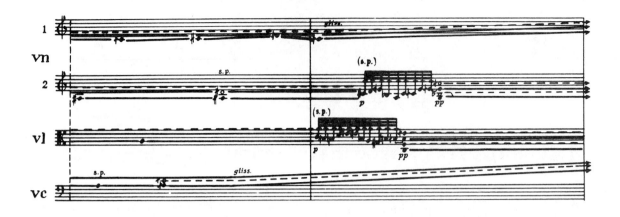

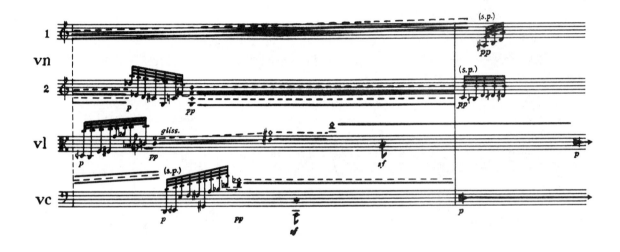

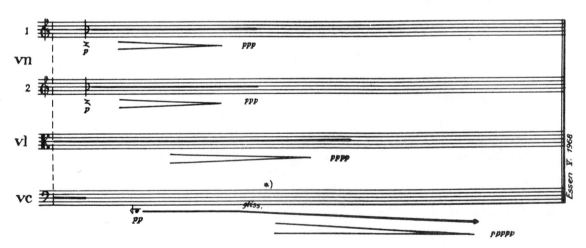

*) during the glissando turn slowly down the turning peg

II. Tu cuerpo, con la sombra violeta de mis manos, era un arcángel de frío
[Through my hands violet shadow, your body was an archangel, cold]

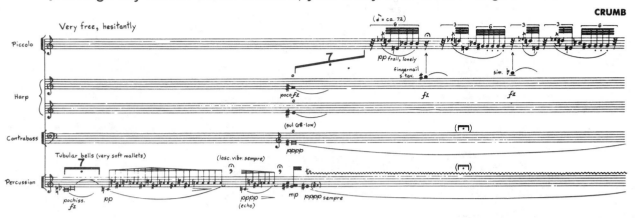

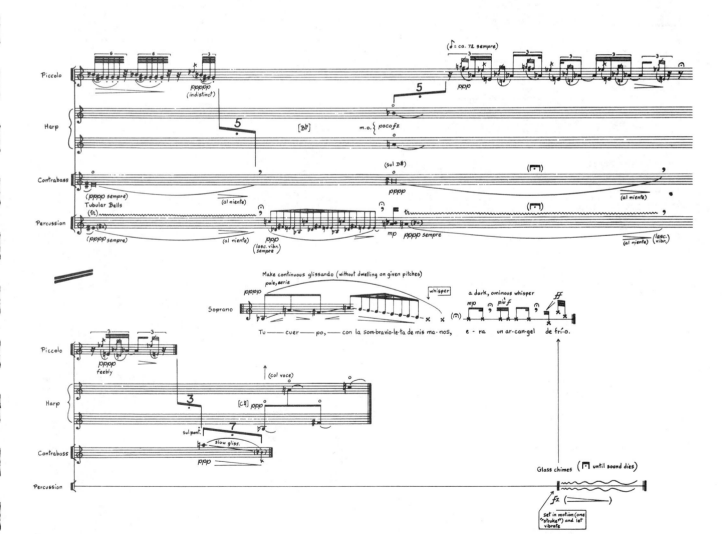

456. Valentine, for solo contrabass

DRUCKMAN

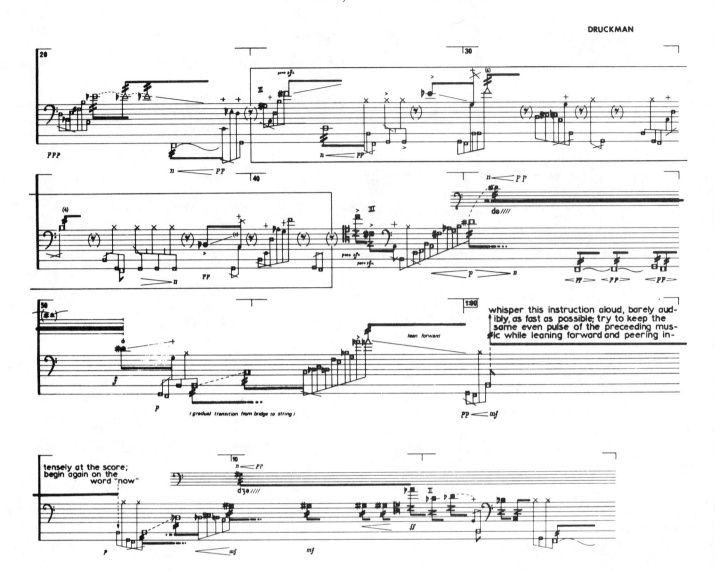

whisper this instruction aloud, barely aud-
ibly, as fast as possible; try to keep the
same even pulse of the preceeding music while leaning forward and peering in-

tensely at the score;
begin again on the
word "now"

(gradual transition from bridge to string)

457. Valentine

Rouse

Solo Flute

458. Six Short Studies, Sixteenth Notes

(fade almost to nothing)

39. Complete Pieces for Analysis IV

Suggestion for Analysis

In the preceding units of Part III, various materials and techniques of the twentieth century appeared in isolation. In the complete pieces in this unit, however, you will find combinations of these materials and techniques within a single work. As a first step, identify these materials and techniques. Then, proceed to analyze this music as you did with the complete pieces in earlier units.

459. Sonatine, Mouv^t II

460. Pour le Piano: Sarabande

461. Préludes, X: La Cathédrale engloutie

Profondément calme (Dans une brume doucement sonore)

Debussy

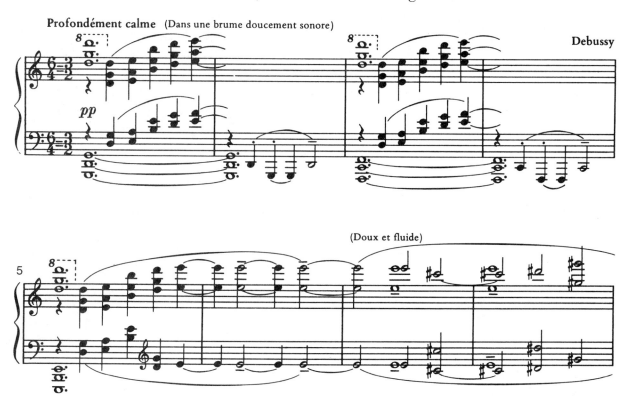

(Doux et fluide)

462. Saudades do Brazil, No. 6: Gavea

Milhaud

Ne garder la Pédale que sur la 1ʳᵉ moitié de la mesure

463. Classical Symphony, op. 25
III

Non troppo allegro

Prokofiev

464. March from The Love of Three Oranges

Prokofiev

465. Ludus Tonalis, Fuga undecima in B (Canon)

Slow (♩ ca.54)

Hindemith

466. Evocations, no. 1

Ruggles

467. Suite für Klavier, op. 25: Menuett

Moderato (♩ = ca.88)

Schönberg

468. Night and Day

Porter

63

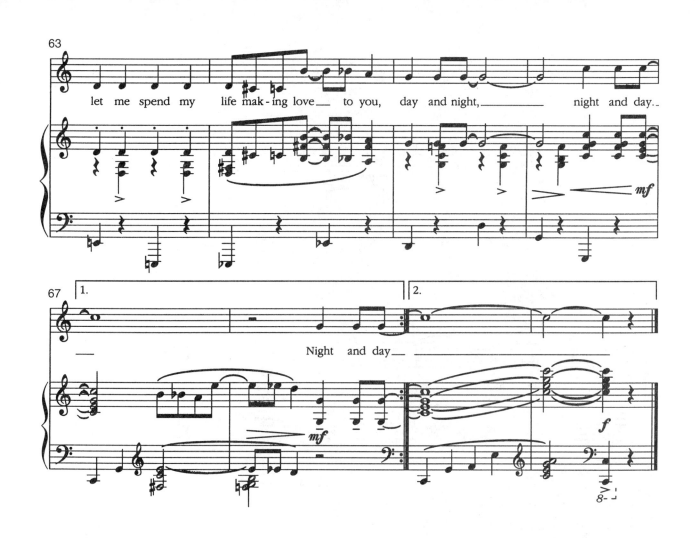

let me spend my life mak-ing love___ to you, day and night,_____ night and day...

67

1.   2.

Night and day___

---

469. Porgy and Bess, "Summertime"

Allegretto semplice   Gershwin

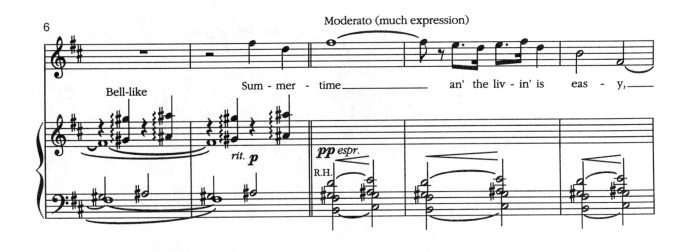

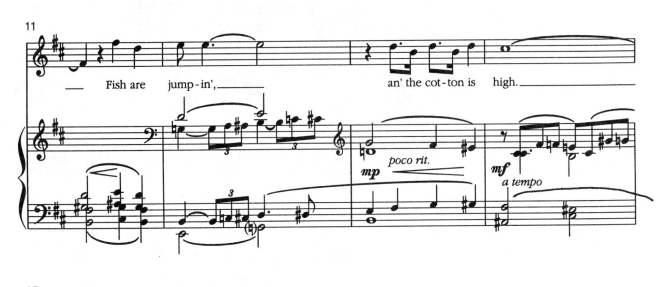

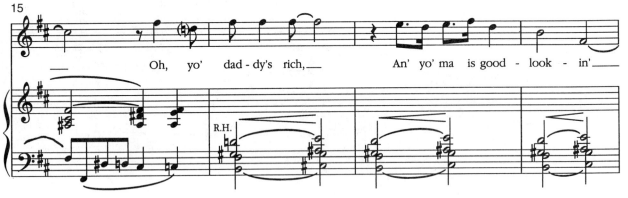

470. Sonata for Two Pianos, II: Theme with Variations

Stravinsky

Variation 1

Variation 2

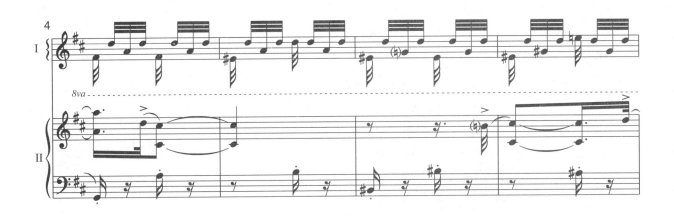

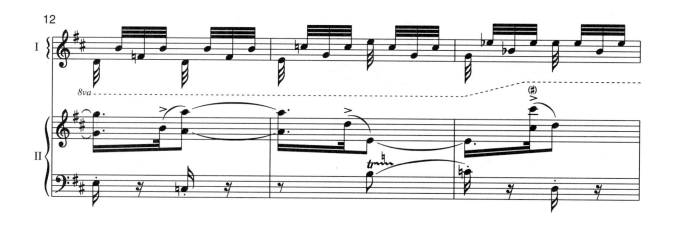

Variation 3

Variation 4
conclusion

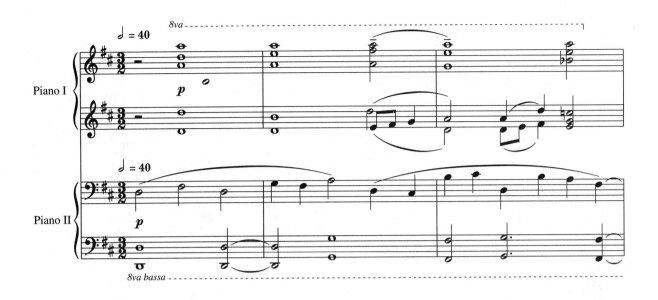

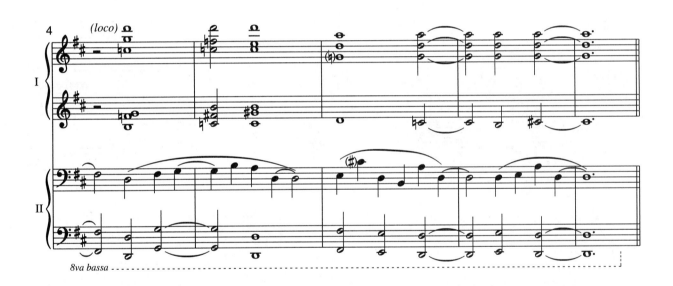

471. Piano Sonata No.2
I

Hindemith

472. Piano Sonata, I

Macmillan

Appendix A

*Checklist for Analysis and Sample Analysis**

All music should be analyzed as fully as possible within the limits of the student's knowledge at any stage of learning. Not only the individual elements but also their interactions should be studied. Following is a checklist of elements that should be included in an analysis.

I. Large and small formal units.
   A. Phrases and periods, if any; phrase-groups; extensions and elisions.
   B. Overall form, including large letters for main sections and formal label if appropriate. Note balance and proportion of sections.
   C. Use of repetition, altered repetition, departure, return, altered return, development, and contrast. Note use of developmental devices.
   D. Elements of unity versus elements of variety.
   E. Stable versus unstable areas (tension versus relaxation).

II. Melodic organization.
   A. Motivic structure, both melodic and rhythmic.
   B. Melodic structure, including departure note and goal note, contour, climax, main structural pitches, range, and tessitura.
   C. Special aspects, such as contrapuntal devices and sequence.

III. Rhythmic organization.
   A. Surface rhythm, meter, harmonic rhythm.
   B. Special devices of rhythmic development.
   C. How is the meter emphasized or obscured?
   D. Tempo.

IV. Harmonic language.
   A. All keys and chords, with Roman numerals and figured bass symbols, or appropriate contemporary nomenclature. How are the key and mode established?
   B. All modulations, indicating type and placement.
   C. All cadences, indicating type and placement.
   D. All nonharmonic tones, by type.
   E. Functional and nonfunctional use of chromaticism.
   F. Use of nonfunctional (linear, coloristic) chords.

V. Sound.
   A. Use of the medium: idiomatic devices, range and tessitura, timbre (color).
   B. Texture.
   C. Dynamics.

VI. Text setting, where appropriate.
   A. Relations between form and/or mood of text and music.
   B. Rhythmic and/or metric relationships.

* Additional sample analyses may be found on pages 11 and 117.

ADDITIONAL QUESTIONS
FOR THE ANALYSIS OF TWENTIETH-CENTURY MUSIC

    I. Tonal centers, if any.
       A. How are they established?
       B. Do they change?
   II. Scalar materials.
       A. What type or types are employed?
       B. Do they change or are they inflected?
 III. Harmonic vocabulary.
       A. What types of chord structures are used?
       B. Is chord succession systematic? If so, how?
  IV. Special metric and rhythmic characteristics.
   V. Refer to page 363 for more comments and questions.

Sample Analysis
Dance

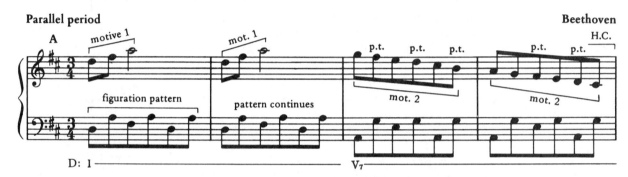

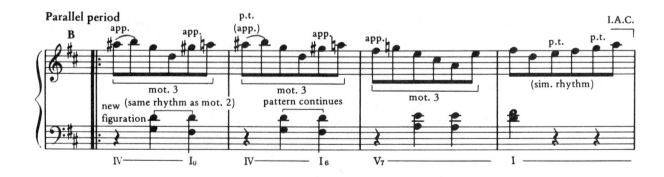

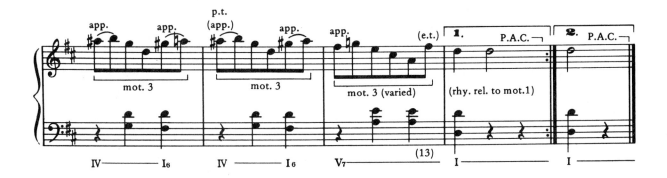

IV ——— I₆   IV ——— I₆   V₇ ——— (13)   I ——— I ———

Observations

    A. Form: simple binary. ‖:A:‖:B:‖

    B. Each section is a parallel period consisting of two four-measure phrases.

    C. There is new motivic material and a new figuration in the B section.

    D. Harmonic rhythm

        1. A section: slow

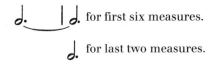 for first six measures.

for last two measures.

        2. B section: faster, slowing at the cadence

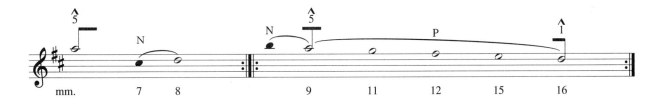 each phrase.

    E. Background rhythmic unit: eighth note motion throughout, passing from the accompanimental figuration in the A section to the melodic material in the B section and coming to rest in the final measure.

    F. Melodic structure.

mm.   7   8   9   11   12   15   16

N = Neighboring motion   P = Passing motion

Appendix B

For Further Reference

Aldwell, Edward, and Carl Schachter. *Harmony and Voice Leading,* 3rd ed. Belmont, CA: Thomson/Schirmer, 2003.

Benjamin, Thomas, Michael Horvit, and Robert Nelson. *Techniques and Materials of Music.* 6th ed. Belmont, CA: Thomson/Schirmer, 2003.

Benjamin, Thomas. *The Craft of Tonal Counterpoint,* 2nd ed. New York: Routledge, 2003.

Benward, Bruce, and Gary White. *Music in Theory and Practice,* 6th ed. New York: McGraw-Hill, 1998.

Berry, Wallace. *Form in Music.* Englewood Cliffs, NJ: Prentice-Hall, 1966.

Clendenning, Jane Piper, and Elizabeth West Marvin. *The Musicians's Guide to Theory and Analysis.* New York: Norton, 2005.

Dallin, Leon. *Twentieth Century Composition,* 3rd ed. Dubuque, IA: William C. Brown, 1974.

Forte, Allen. *The Structure of Atonal Music.* New Haven, CT: Yale University Press, 1977.

Gauldin, Robert. *Harmonic Practice in Tonal Music,* 2nd ed. New York: Norton, 2004.

Gauldin, Robert. *A Practical Approach to Eighteenth-Century Counterpoint.* Prospect Heights, IL: Waveland Press, 1995.

Green, Douglass. *Form in Tonal Music: An Introduction to Analysis,* 2nd ed. New York: Holt, Rinehart, and Winston, 1979.

Kennan, Kent. *Counterpoint: Based on Eighteenth Century Practice,* 4th ed. Englewood Cliffs, NJ: Prentice-Hall, 1999.

Kostka, Stefan. *Materials and Techniques of Twentieth-Century Music.* 2nd ed. Englewood Cliffs, NJ: Prentice-Hall, 1999.

Kostka, Stefan, and Dorothy Payne. *Tonal Harmony, with an Introduction to Twentieth Century Music,* 5th ed. Boston: McGraw-Hill, 2004.

Laitz, Stephen G. *The Complete Musician: An Integrated Approach to Tonal Theory, Listening, and Analysis.* New York: Oxford University Press, 2003.

Lester, Joel. *Analytic Approach to Twentieth-Century Music.* New York: Norton, 1989.

Ottman, Robert W. *Elementary Harmony,* 5th ed. Englewood Cliffs, NJ: Prentice-Hall, 1998.

——*Advanced Harmony,* 5th ed. Englewood Cliffs, NJ: Prentice-Hall, 2000.

Persichetti, Vincent. *Twentieth-Century Harmony.* New York: Norton, 1961.

Piston, Walter. *Harmony,* 5th ed. Revised and expanded by Mark De Voto. New York: Norton, 1987.

Roig-Francoli, Miguel. *Harmony in Context.* Boston: McGraw-Hill, 2003.

Spencer, Peter, and Peter M. Temko. *A Practical Approach to the Study of Form in Music.* Prospect Heights, IL: Waveland Press, 1994.

Steinke, Greg. *Bridge to 20th-Century Music.* Boston: Allyn and Bacon, 1999.

Strauss, Joseph. *Introduction to Post-Tonal Theory,* 3rd ed. Englewood Cliffs, NJ: Prentice-Hall, 2005.

Appendix C

Textbook Correlation Chart

CHAPTER	ALDWELL	BENJAMIN 6th Edition	BENWARD	CLENDENNING	GAULDIN 2nd Edition
1	6	II:2	I:4	7	9
2	6	II:3	I:4	7,12	9
3	6	II:4	I:11	7,12	9
			II:10		
4	9	II:5,6	I:4	7	15
5	10	II:8	I:9	15	16
6	7	II:9	I:9	7	13,15
7	9	II:10	I:4	7	15
8	8	II:11	I:11	7	13
9	19	II:12	I:9	15	16
10	11,15	II:13	I:4	16	18
11	15	II:14	I:4	7	13
12	22	II:15	II:4	24	28
13	12	II:17	II:4	7	17
14	23	II:18	I:12	7	21
			II:4		
15	24	II:19	I:13	7	17
17	25	III:1	I:15	19,21	25
18	26	III:2	I:14	22	27
20	29	III:3	II:13		32
21	28	III:4	II:5	25	29
22–24	29	III:5	II:6,11		30
25	32	III:6	II:13		34,40
26	27	III:7	II:10		35
27	31	IV:4	II:10		37,39
29		V:19	II:2,3		
30		IV:4	II:10	7	App. 4
31		IV:5	II:1,14	30	App. 2
32		IV:7	II:14,15		
33		IV:6	II:14	30	App. 2
34		IV:8	II:15		
35		IV:9	II:15		
36		IV:10	II:16	30-32	
37		IV:11	II:16	33-34	
38		IV:12	II:POSTLUDE	37	II:14,16

Textbook Correlation Chart

CHAPTER	KOTSKA	LAITZ	OTTMAN*	PISTON 5th Edition	ROIGH-FRANCOLI
1	6	5	I:4,5	2,3,4	E,2
2	6	5	I:4,5	2,3,4,5	E,2
3	6,12	5,6,8	I:13 II:10	15	E,12
4	6	5,13	I:6	2,3,4,55,13	E,3
5	9	11	I:9	10	E,9
6	7	5,9	I:9	6	E,4
7	6,7	5,13	I:10	2,3,4,5	E,10
8	12	5,6,10	I:13	15	E,12
9	9	11	I:9	10	E,9
10	6	5,15,16	I:14	2,3,4,5	E,14
11	6	5	I:10	2,6	E,13
12	21	24	I:16	4,5	22
13	13	6	I:13	23	E
14	13	6,10	II:2	23	E
15	14	6	II:6	23	E,13-15
17	16,17	21	I:18	16,17	16-18
18	18	22	I:18 II:1	14,20	19
20		25	II:2	21	
21	22	26	II:7	26	23
22–24	23,24	27	II:7,8,9	27,28	23
25	25		II:3,7,9	14,21,26,27	24-5
26	26		II:10	24	
27	27	31	II:10	24	27
29					21
30			II:13	31	27
31			II:13	30	
32			II:13,15	31	
33			II:13	31	
34			II:13,15	31	
35			II:15	31	
36			II:16	32	
37			II:16	32	
38			II:16		

*"I" refers to *Elementary Harmony*; "II" refers to *Advanced Harmony.*

ACKNOWLEDGMENTS
(These Acknowledgments constitute a continuation of the copyright page.)

Unit 13   *Blue Moon* by Richard Rodgers and Lorenz Hart. © 1934 (Renewed) Metro-Goldwyn-Mayer Inc. All Rights controlled by EMI Robbins Catalog Inc. All Rights Reserved. Excerpt used by Permission of Alfred Publishing Company, Inc., Van Nuys, CA 91410.

Unit 17   *Can I Forget You?* by Jerome Kern and Oscar Hammerstein II. © 1937 (Renewed) Universal-Polygram International Publishing, Inc. All Rights Reserved. Used by Permission of Alfred Publishing Company, Inc., Van Nuys, CA 91410.

Unit 19   *You Took Advantage of Me* from *Present Arms*. Words by Lorenz Hart. Music by Richard Rodgers. Copyright © 1928 by Williamson Music and The Estate of Lorenz Hart in the United States. Copyright Renewed. All Rights on behalf of The Estate of Lorenz Hart Administered by WB Music Corp. International Copyright Secured. All Rights Reserved. Used by Permission of Hal Leonard Corporation.

Unit 20   *The Girl Friend* by Richard Rodgers and Lorenz Hart. © 1926 (Renewed) Warner Bos. Inc. Rights for Extended Renewal Term in the U.S. controlled by The Estate of Lorenz Hart (administered by WB Music Corp.) and The Family Trust U/W Richard Rodgers and The Family Trust U/W Dorothy F. Rodgers (administered by Williamson Music). All Rights Reserved. Excerpt used by Permission of Alfred Publishing Company, Inc., Van Nuys, CA 91410.

Unit 27   *Lover* from the Paramount Picture *Love Me Tonight*. Words by Lorenz Hart. Music by Richard Rodgers. Copyright © 1932, 1933 (renewed 1959, 1960) by Famous Music Corporation. International Copyright Secured. All Rights Reserved. Excerpt used by Permission of Hal Leonard Corporation.

Unit 28   *Smoke Gets in Your Eyes* by Jerome Kern and Otto Harbach. © 1933 (Renewed) Universal-Polygram International Publishing, Inc. All Rights Reserved. Used by Permission of Alfred Publishing Company, Inc., Van Nuys, CA 91410.

Unit 30   *Symphony No. 2*, Op. 30 (excerpt), by Howard Hanson. Copyright © 1932 by the Eastman School of Music. Copyright renewed. All Rights Reserved. Reprinted by permission Carl Fischer, LLC.

           Mysterious Mountain, I, Andante (excerpt), by Alan Hovhaness. Copyright © 1944 (Renewed) by Associated Music Publishers, Inc. (BMI). International Copyright Secured. All Rights Reserved. Reprinted by Permission of G. Schimer, Inc.

           Slaughter on Tenth Avenue from *On Your Toes* by Richard Rodgers. Copyright © 1936 by Williamson Music. Copyright Renewed. International Copyright Secured. All Rights Reserved. Used by Permission of Hal Leonard Corporation.

           September Song (excerpt) from *Knickerbocker Holiday* by Kurt Weill and Maxwell Anderson. Copyright © Chappell & Co. Warner Bros. Publications.

           Prelude to a Kiss by Duke Ellington, Irving Mills, and Irving Gordon. © 1938 (Renewed) EMI Mills Music, Inc. and Famous Music Corporation in U.S. All Rights outside U.S. controlled by EMI Mills Music, Inc. All Rights Reserved. Excerpt used by Permission of Warner Bros. Publications U.S. Inc., Miami, FL, 33014.

           Jordu by Duke Jordan. Copyright © Slow Dancing Music and Tamara Shad, 3060 Deep Canyon Drive, Beverly Hills, CA 90210. Used by permission. All rights reserved.

Unit 31   *Ten Preludes for the Piano*, No. 1 (excerpt), by Carlos Chavez. Copyright © 1940 (Renewed) by G. Schirmer, Inc. (ASCAP). International Copyright Secured. All Rights Reserved. Reprinted by Permission.

           Valse (excerpt) by Francis Poulenc. Copyright © 1920 Editions Max Eschig. Used by Permission of Theodore Presser Company.

           Ceremony of Carols, No. 8, by Benjamin Britten. © Copyright 1943 by Boosey & Co., Ltd. Copyright renewed. Reprinted by permission of Boosey & Hawkes, Inc.

Suite für Klavier, Op. 25, "Gavotte" by Arnold Schönberg. Used by permission of Belmont Music Publishers.

Cinque Frammenti di Saffo by Luigi Dallapiccola. © Copyright 1943 by Edizione Suivini Zerboni S.P.A. Reprinted by permission of Sugar-Melodi Inc.

Drei Lieder, op. 25, No. 1, by Anton Webern. © 1956 by Universal Edition A.G., Wien. © renewed. All Rights Reserved. Used by permission of European American Music Distributors LLC, U.S. and Canadian agent for Universal Edition A.G., Wien.

Unit 38   *Klavierstücke*, No. 2 (excerpt) by Karlheinz Stockhausen. © 1954 by Universal Edition (London) Ltd., London. © renewed. All Rights Reserved. Used by permission of European American Music Distributors LLC, U.S. and Canadian agent for Universal Edition A.G., Wien.

String Quartet (excerpt) by Witold Lutoslawski. Copyright © 1967, 1993 Chester Music Limited for the world except Poland, Albania, Bulgaria, the territories of former Czechoslovakia, Romania, Hungary, and the whole territory of the former USSR, Cuba, China, Vietnam, and North Korea, where the copyright is held by Polskie Wydawnictwo Muzyczyne, Krakow, Poland. International Copyright Secured. All Rights Reserved. Reprinted by Permission G. Schirmer, Inc. U.S. Agent.

String Quartet No. 2 (excerpt) by Krzysztof Penderecki. © 1961 (Renewed) EMI Deshon Music, Inc. and PWM Editions. All Rights Reserved. Excerpt used by Permission of Warner Bros. Publications U.S. Inc., Miami, FL, 33014.

Madrigals, Book IV, No. 2, by George Crumb. © 1971 by C. F. Peters Corporation. Used by permlsslon.

Valentine for Solo Contrabass (excerpt) by Jacob Druckman. Copyright © 1970 MCA Music Publishing. International copyright secured. All rights reserved. Boosey & Hawkes.

Valentine by Christopher Rouse. © Copyright 1996 by Hendon Music, Inc., a Boosey & Hawkes company. Reprinted by permission of Boosey & Hawkes, Inc.

Six Short Studes, "Sixteenth Notes," by David Horne. © Copyright 1997 by Boosey & Hawkes Music Publishers Ltd. Reprinted by permission of Boosey & Hawkes, Inc.

Unit 39   *Classical Symphony*, Op. 25, "Minuet," by Sergei Prokofiev. Copyright © Boosey & Hawkes.

Love of Three Oranges, "March," by Sergei Prokofiev. © Copyright 1922, 1935, 1978 by Hawkes & Son (London) Ltd. Copyright Renewed. Reprinted by permission of Boosey & Hawkes, Inc.

Ludus Tonalis, "Fuga Undecima in B," by Paul Hindemith. © by Schott Music International 1943. © renewed. All Rights Reserved. Used by permission of European American Music Distributors LLC, sole U.S. and Canadian agent for Schott Musik International.

Evocations, No. 1, by Carl Ruggles. © 1956 American Music Edition Theodore Presser Company, sole representative. Used by Permission.

Suite für Klavier, Op. 25, "Menuett," by Arnold Schönberg. Used by permission of Belmont Music Publishers.

Piano Sonata, I, by James Macmillan. © Copyright 1992 by Boosey & Hawkes Music Publishers Ltd. Reprinted by permission of Boosey & Hawkes, Inc.

Night and Day by Cole Porter. Copyright © 1932 (Renewed) Warner Bros. Inc. All Rights Reserved. Used by Permission of Alfred Publishing Company, Inc., Van Nuys, CA 91410.

Summertime by George Gershwin, Dubose and Dorothy Heyward, and Ira Gershwin. © 1935 (Renewed 1962) George Gershwin Music, Ira Gershwin Music, and Dubose and Dorothy Heyward Memorial Fund Publishing. All Rights Administered by WB Music Corp. All Rights Reserved. Used by Permission of Alfred Publishing Company, Inc., Van Nuys, CA 91410.

Sonata for Two Pianos, II: Theme with Variations by Igor Stravinsky. © Copyright 1945 in the USA by Boosey & Hawkes, Inc. Copyright Renewed. Reprinted by permission.

Piano Sonata, No.2, I by Paul Hindemith. © by Schott Musik International 1936. © renewed. All Rights Reserved. Used by permission of European American Music Distributors LLC, sole U.S. and Canadian agent for Schott Musik International.

Index of Composers and Their Compositions

(Numbers in **bold** refer to *selection* numbers.)

Beethoven, Ludwig von, *continued*
    Symphony No. 2, op. 36 **67, 137, 209**
    Symphony No. 3, op. 55 **82**
    Symphony No. 4, op. 60 **21, 184**
    Symphony No. 5, op. 67 **8, 15, 44, 127, 312**
    Symphony No. 6, op. 68 **133, 139**
    Symphony No. 7, op. 92 **77, 223, 244, 316**
    Thirty-Two Variations, Var. 30 **280**
    Trio, op. 1, no. 1 **173, 179**; no. 3 **95, 195**
    Trio, op. 11 **190, 324**
    Trio, op. 70, no. 2 **5**
    Trio, op. 70, no. 1 **319**
    Trio, op. 97 **38**
    Trio, op. 121A **55**
Bellini, Vincenzo (1801–1835)
    I Puritani, Act II, scene 3 **254**
Berg, Alban (1885–1935)
    Four Songs, op. 2, no. 3 **389**
    Wozzeck, Act II **426, 428**
Berger, Arthur (1912–2003)
    Two Episodes, I **441**
Bizet, Georges (1838–1875)
    Carmen, Act II, Entr'acte **140**
Bononcini, Giovanni (1670–1747)
    Deh più a me non vàscondete **226**
Brahms, Johannes (1833–1897)
    Ballade, op. 10, no. 4 **145**
    Chorale Prelude on Oh wie selig seid
        ihr doch, ihr Frommen **370**
    Der Tod, das ist die kühle Nacht,
        op. 96, no. 1 **341**
    Intermezzo, op. 76, no. 4 **301**
    Intermezzo in A major, op. 118, no. 2 **263**
    Liebeslieder Walzer, op. 52, no. 4 **257**
    Quintet, op. 115 **222**
    Romance, op. 118, no. 5 **100**
    Symphony No. 3, op. 90 **125**
    Symphony No. 4, op. 98 **92, 128**
    Variations on a Theme by Handel,
        var. 20 **343**
    Waltz, op. 39 **238**; no. 15 **228**
    Wenn du nur zuweilen lächelst, op. 57,
        no. 2 **311**
    Wie bist du meine Königen, op. 32,
        no. 9 **322**
    Wie Melodien zieht es mir, op. 105 **266**
Britten, Benjamin (1913–1976)
    Ceremony of Carols, no. 8 **395**
Brubeck, Dave (1920–   )
    Blue Rondo à la Turk **431**
    Strange Meadowlark **439**
Buxtehude, Dietrich (1637–1707)
    Passacaglia **81**

Byrd, William (1543–1623)
    Pavana "The Earle of Salisbury" **115**

Casella, Alfredo (1883–1947)
    Siciliana **400**
Chávez, Carlos (1899–1978)
    Ten Preludes, no. 1 **391**
Chopin, Frédéric (1810–1849)
    Mazurka, op. 6, no. 1 **340**
    Mazurka, op. 7, no. 2 **214**
    Mazurka, op. 17, no. 1 **28**
    Mazurka, op. 24, no. 3 **36**
    Mazurka, op. 33, no. 2 **57**
    Mazurka, op. 67, no. 2 **201**
    Mazurka, op. post 67, no. 2 **353**
    Polens Grabgesang, op. 74 **6**
    Prelude, op. 28, no. 6 **270**; no. 9 **348**;
        no. 15 **332**; no. 20 **264**; no. 22 **303**
    Valse, op. 69, no. 1 **202**
    Valse Brillante, op. 34, no. 1 **330**; no. 3 **203**
    Valse (Posthumous) **7**
    Zwei Leichen **54**
Copland, Aaron (1900–1990)
    The Young Pioneers **405**
Corelli, Arcangelo (1653–1713)
    Sonata for Violin and Continuo, op. 5,
        no. 9 **93**
Couperin, François (1668–1733)
    Carnival **9**
    Le Petit Rien **48**
Cowell, Henry (1897–1965)
    The Irishman Dances **404**
    Tiger **429**
Crüger, Johann (1598–1662)
    Herzliebster Jesu, was hast du
        verbrochen **85**
Crumb, George (1929–   )
    Madrigals, Book IV **455**
Czerny, Carl (1791–1857)
    Sonatina, op. 792, no. 8 **2**

Dallapiccola, Luigi (1904–1975)
    Cinque Frammenti di Saffo **450**
Dandrieu, Jean (1682–1738)
    Les Fifres **49**
Daquin, Louis-Claude (1694–1772)
    La Joyeuse **111**
Debussy, Claude (1862–1918)
    Pelléas et Mélisande, Act I,
        scene 1 **382**
    Pelléas et Mélisande, Act II,
        scene I **415**
    Pour le Piano: Sarabande **460**

(Numbers in **bold** refer to *selection* numbers.)

(Numbers in **bold** refer to *selection* numbers.)

(Numbers in **bold** refer to *selection* numbers.)

Index of Complete Pieces
(Including Examples of Small Forms)
(* denotes contrapuntal example)

(Numbers in **bold** refer to *selection* numbers.)